SCIENTOLOGY® 8-8008

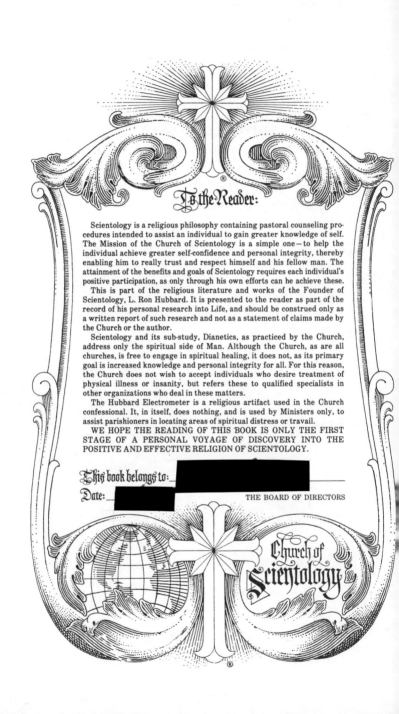

To the Reader:

Scientology is a religious philosophy containing pastoral counseling procedures intended to assist an individual to gain greater knowledge of self. The Mission of the Church of Scientology is a simple one—to help the individual achieve greater self-confidence and personal integrity, thereby enabling him to really trust and respect himself and his fellow man. The attainment of the benefits and goals of Scientology requires each individual's positive participation, as only through his own efforts can he achieve these.

This is part of the religious literature and works of the Founder of Scientology, L. Ron Hubbard. It is presented to the reader as part of the record of his personal research into Life, and should be construed only as a written report of such research and not as a statement of claims made by the Church or the author.

Scientology and its sub-study, Dianetics, as practiced by the Church, address only the spiritual side of Man. Although the Church, as are all churches, is free to engage in spiritual healing, it does not, as its primary goal is increased knowledge and personal integrity for all. For this reason, the Church does not wish to accept individuals who desire treatment of physical illness or insanity, but refers these to qualified specialists in other organizations who deal in these matters.

The Hubbard Electrometer is a religious artifact used in the Church confessional. It, in itself, does nothing, and is used by Ministers only, to assist parishioners in locating areas of spiritual distress or travail.

WE HOPE THE READING OF THIS BOOK IS ONLY THE FIRST STAGE OF A PERSONAL VOYAGE OF DISCOVERY INTO THE POSITIVE AND EFFECTIVE RELIGION OF SCIENTOLOGY.

This book belongs to: _____

Date: _____

THE BOARD OF DIRECTORS

Church of Scientology

SCIENTOLOGY® 8-8008

by
L. Ron Hubbard

PUBLICATIONS ORGANIZATION
UNITED STATES

Published by
The Church of Scientology of California
Publications Organization U.S.
(The Church of Scientology of California
is a non-profit organization)
2723 West Temple Street
Los Angeles, California 90026

The Church of Scientology is a non-profit organization.
Scientology is an applied religious philosophy.
Dianetics ® and Scientology ® are registered names.

Ninth Printing, 1974

THE E-METER IS NOT INTENDED OR EFFECTIVE FOR THE
DIAGNOSIS, TREATMENT OR PREVENTION OF ANY DISEASE

REVISED AND REPRINTED SEPTEMBER 1976

A Dianetics Publication. Dianetics is the trademark of L. Ron Hubbard in respect of his published works.

ISBN 0-88404-008-9

Printed in the United States of America

CONTENTS

Important Note

In studying Dianetics and Scientology be very, very certain you never go past a word you do not fully understand.

The only reason a person gives up a study or becomes confused or unable to learn is that he or she has gone past a word or phrase that was not understood.

Trying to read past a misunderstood word results in mental "fogginess" and difficulty in comprehending the passages which follow. If you find yourself experiencing this, return to the last portion you understood easily, locate the misunderstood word and get it defined correctly—and then go on.

DIANETICS®: From the Greek dia (through) and noos *(soul), thus "through the soul"; a system for the analysis, control and development of human thought which also provides techniques for increased ability, rationality, and freedom from the discovered single source of aberrations and psychosomatic ills. Introduced May, 1950, with publication of* Dianetics: The Modern Science of Mental Health *by L. Ron Hubbard.*

SCIENTOLOGY® is an applied religious philosophy and technology resolving problems of the spirit, life and thought; discovered, developed and organized by L. Ron Hubbard as a result of his earlier Dianetic discoveries. Coming from the Latin, scio *(knowing) and the Greek* logos *(study), Scientology means "knowing how to know" or "the study of wisdom."*

FOREWORD

THE work contained in this book is the result of 25 years' investigation of electronics as they apply to knowledge and human thinking by L. Ron Hubbard.

In his youth, Hubbard had the good fortune to know Commander Thompson (M.C.), U.S.N., who had studied with Sigmund Freud in Vienna. Stimulated by Freud's investigatory spirit and by the encouragement of the late Commander Thompson, and equipped with considerable personal experience in the Orient with phenomena not generally known in the Western World, Hubbard bent the exactitudes of Occidental engineering to the investigation and practical application of such data to the human mind.

His studies of the subject were extremely broad and varied. They included such things as expeditions to investigate the ethnology of twelve widely-separated primitive cultures, an intensive survey of the endocrine system, the study of early writers and philosophers on the subject of mankind and epistemology, also the direct study of his forte, nuclear physics, as it might be found to apply to the human intellect.

In addition to Sigmund Freud and Commander Thompson, he has credited the following persons as source material:

Anaxagoras	Thomas Jefferson
Aristotle	Jesus of Nazareth
Roger Bacon	Count Alfred Korzybski
Buddha	James Clerk Maxwell
Charcot	Mohammed
Confucius	Lao Tsze
René Descartes	van Leeuwenhoek
Will Durant	Lucretius
Euclid	Isaac Newton
Michael Faraday	Thomas Paine
William James	Plato

| Socrates | The Vedic Hymns |
| Herbert Spencer | Voltaire |

L. Ron Hubbard's work has excited interest and comment throughout the world, and its more elementary forms are to-day taught in at least two leading universities. Some of his earlier discoveries have become accepted fact by the medical profession and his methodology is now in use in several institutions.

Some think of his work as the only significant enlargement of the field of the mind since Freud's papers in the late 19th century; others think of it as the Western world's first workable organization of Eastern philosophy. It has been called by two of the leading writers in America: "The most significant advance of mankind in the 20th century."

Many lay writers have sensationalized these developments in the extreme, and others have levelled against this work the bitterest of condemnations: whether bad or good, no development in the field of the mind for many centuries has excited as much interest.

L. Ron Hubbard is himself a man of considerable energy and of extremely wide interests. He has written fiction under many of his pen-names; and, indeed, financed and supported his own investigations (which have cost in the hundreds of thousands of dollars) with his own pen. His interests do not lie in the field of practice but in the field of continued investigation.

Probably no philosopher of modern times has had the popularity and appeal of Hubbard or such startling successes within his own lifetime. And mankind has had no better friend.

THE EDITOR

THE FACTORS

(Summation of the considerations and examinations of the human spirit and the material universe completed between A.D. 1923 and 1953.)

1. *Before the beginning was a Cause and the entire purpose of the Cause was the creation of effect.*
2. *In the beginning and forever is the decision and the decision is TO BE.*
3. *The first action of beingness is to assume a viewpoint.*
4. *The second action of beingness is to extend from the viewpoint, points to view, which are dimension points.*
5. *Thus there is space created, for the definition of space is: viewpoint of dimension. And the purpose of a dimension point is space and a point of view.*
6. *The action of a dimension point is reaching and withdrawing.*
7. *And from the viewpoint to the dimension points there are connection and interchange. Thus new dimension points are made. Thus there is communication.*
8. *And thus there is light.*
9. *And thus there is energy.*
10. *And thus there is life.*
11. *But there are other viewpoints and these viewpoints outthrust points to view. And there comes about an interchange amongst viewpoints; but the interchange is never otherwise than in terms of exchanging dimension points.*
12. *The dimension point can be moved by the viewpoint, for the viewpoint, in addition to creative ability and consideration, possesses volition and potential independence of action; and the viewpoint, viewing dimension points, can change in relation to its own or other dimension points or viewpoints. Thus comes about all the fundamentals there are to motion.*

13. *The dimension points are each and every one, whether large or small, solid. And they are solid solely because the viewpoints say they are solid.*

14. *Many dimension points combine into larger gases, fluids or solids. Thus there is matter. But the most valued point is admiration, and admiration is so strong its absence alone permits persistence.*

15. *The dimension point can be different from other dimension points and thus can possess an individual quality. And many dimension points can possess a similar quality, and others can possess a similar quality unto themselves. Thus comes about the quality of classes of matter.*

16. *The viewpoint can combine dimension points into forms and the forms can be simple or complex and can be at different distances from the viewpoints and so there can be combinations of form. And the forms are capable of motion and the viewpoints are capable of motion and so there can be motion of forms.*

17. *And the opinion of the viewpoint regulates the consideration of the forms, their stillness or their motion, and these considerations consist of assignment of beauty or ugliness to the forms and these considerations alone are art.*

18. *It is the opinion of the viewpoints that some of these forms should endure. Thus there is survival.*

19. *And the viewpoint can never perish; but the form can perish.*

20. *And the many viewpoints, interacting, become dependent upon one another's forms and do not choose to distinguish completely the ownership of dimension points and so comes about a dependency upon the dimension points and upon the other viewpoints.*

21. *From this comes a consistency of viewpoint of the interaction of dimension points and this, regulated, is TIME.*

22. *And there are universes.*

23. *The universes, then, are three in number: the universe created by one viewpoint, the universe created by every*

other viewpoint, the universe created by the mutual action of viewpoints which is agreed to be upheld—the physical universe.

24. *And the viewpoints are never seen. And the viewpoints consider more and more that the dimension points are valuable. And the viewpoints try to become the anchor points and forget that they can create more points and space and forms. Thus comes about scarcity. And the dimension points can perish and so the viewpoints assume that they, too, can perish.*

25. *Thus comes about death.*

26. *The manifestations of pleasure and pain, of thought, emotion and effort, of thinking, of sensation, of affinity, reality, communication, of behaviour and being are thus derived and the riddles of our universe are apparently contained and answered herein.*

27. *There is beingness, but Man believes there is only becomingness.*

28. *The resolution of any problem posed hereby is the establishment of viewpoints and dimension points, the betterment of condition and concourse amongst dimension points, and, thereby, viewpoints, and the remedy of abundance or scarcity in all things, pleasant or ugly, by the rehabilitation of the ability of the viewpoint to assume points of view, and create and uncreate, neglect, start, change and stop dimension points of any kind at the determinism of the viewpoint. Certainty in all three universes must be regained, for certainty, not data, is knowledge.*

29. *In the opinion of the viewpoint, any beingness, any thing, is better than no thing, any effect is better than no effect, any universe better than no universe, any particle better than no particle, but the particle of admiration is best of all.*

30. *And above these things there might be speculation only. And below these things there is the playing of the game. But these things which are written here Man can experi-*

ence and know. And some may care to teach these things and some may care to use them to assist those in distress and some may desire to employ them to make individuals and organizations more able and so give to Earth a culture of which we can be proud.

Humbly tendered as a gift to Man by
L. Ron Hubbard,
April 23, 1953.

THE BEINGNESS OF MAN

Any study of knowledge could not but be intimately connected with the beingness of Man and the earliest axioms of Scientology began to predict and the later developments eventually discovered the highest level data so far obtained on the identity and capability of life.

The well-beingness and, indeed, the continued survival of mankind depend upon an exact knowledge of his own capabilities; and thus, more particularly, of his own relationship to knowledge itself.

The basic goal of Man which embraces all his activities is apparently survival. Survival might be defined as an impulse to persist through time, in space, as matter and energy.

The impulse to survival is found to contain eight sub-impulses. These are, first, the urge to survive as self; second, the urge to survive through sex in the procreation of children; third, the impulse to survive as a group; fourth, the impulse to survive as mankind itself; fifth, the urge to survive as animal life; sixth, the impulse to survive as the material universe of matter, energy, space and time; seventh, the impulse to survive as a spirit; and eighth, the impulse to survive as what may be called Supreme Being.

The above sub-impulses are called *dynamics;* combined, they form the overall urge towards survival, but each one of itself plays its important role, both in the individual and in the wider sphere named as a part of each impulse. Thus we see the inter-dependency of the individual with the family, with the group, with the species, with life-forms, with the material universe itself, with spirits, and with God; and we see the dependency of each one of these entities upon the individual as a part of it.

The human mind might be conceived to be the recorder, computer and solver of problems relating to survival.

Scientology introduces new and more workable ways of

thinking about things. It has found that an absolute is unobtainable; neither zero nor infinity are as themselves discoverable in a real universe but, as absolutes, may be posed as symbols for an abstraction which could be supposed to exist but which does not exist in fact. Therefore, there would be no absolute good and no absolute evil. A thing to be "good" would depend on the viewpoint of the observer, and the same condition would exist for "bad."

Several new concepts germane to the fields of science and humanities almost independent of its own work have been introduced by Scientology. The first of these is the proper definition of a static. The next is the first actual definition of zero and its differentiation from infinity in terms of mathematics. Another is the basic definition of space which hitherto was omitted from the field of physics except in terms of time and energy.

An optimum solution to any problem would be that solution which brought the greatest benefits to the greatest number of dynamics. The poorest solution would be that solution which brought the fewest benefits to the least number of dynamics. And here a benefit would be defined as that which would enhance survival. Activities which brought minimal survival to a lesser number of dynamics and damaged the survival of a greater number of dynamics could not be considered rational activities.

While there could be no absolute right or absolute wrong, a right action would depend upon its assisting the survival of the dynamics immediately concerned; a wrong action would impede the survival of the dynamics concerned.

Thought is subdivisible into data. A datum would be anything of which one could become aware, whether the thing existed or whether he created it.

Creativeness could be found to exceed existence itself; by observation and definition it is discoverable that thought does not necessarily have to be preceded by data, but can create data. Imagination can then create without reference to pre-existing states, and is not necessarily dependent upon experi-

6

ence or data and does not necessarily combine these for its products. Imagination could be classified as the ability to create or forecast a future or to create, change or destroy a present or past.

Cause is motivated by the future.

Scientology as it applies to life is seen as a study in statics and kinetics, which is to say a study of the interplay between no motion and all motion, or less motion and more motion.

In thought itself at its highest range, we discover the only true static known. In physics a static is represented as a body at rest but it is known in physics that a body at rest is yet an equilibrium of forces and is itself in motion if only on the level of molecular motion. A true static would contain no motion, no time, no space and no wavelength. To this static in Scientology is assigned the mathematical symbol *theta*. This designation means solely a theoretical static of distinct and precisely defined qualities with certain potentials.

The all-motion or more-motion kinetic is termed MEST. This word represents the material universe, or any universe. It is combined from the first letters of the four words: matter, energy, space and time.

The interplay between theta and mest results in activities known as life, and causes the animation of living life forms. In the absence of an interplay, the life form is dead.

The beingness of Man, by which is meant homo sapiens, derives its impulse toward thought and action from theta and takes its material form in mest.

Man, homo sapiens, is a composite being of four distinct and divisible actualities: these parts are termed the thetan, the memory banks, the genetic entity and the body.

The thetan, which will be described later in greater detail, has the impulse of theta itself and can exist in matter, energy, space and time, but derives its impulse from the potential of theta itself and has certain definite goals and behaviour characteristics of its own.

The standard memory banks and the reactive memory banks compose the memory banks of homo sapiens. These in the analogy of an electronic computer, are the file system. The standard banks can be said to contain data of which Man is easily and analytically aware and the reactive banks are those which contain stimulus-response, in other words experience the action of which is below the level of his awareness. The content of the reactive banks was received during moments of lessened awareness such as the unconsciousness of early life in times of weariness, severe pain or heavy emotional stress, such data operating automatically thereafter to command the person without his consent. The standard memory banks are those in which experience is stored for use in the estimation of the effort necessary for survival and are concerned with analytical thought. There is an additional storage of memory itself in a purer form than in these banks, but this memory is contained in the capabilities of the thetan.

The genetic entity is that beingness not dissimilar to the thetan which has carried forward and developed the body from its earliest moments along the evolutionary line on earth and which through experience, necessity and natural selection, has employed the counter-efforts of the environment to fashion an organism of the type best fitted for survival, limited only by the abilities of the genetic entity. The goal of the genetic entity is survival on a much grosser plane of materiality.

The body itself is a carbon-oxygen engine which runs at a temperature of 98.6°F. on low combustion fuel, generally derived from other life forms. The body is directly monitored by the genetic entity in activities such as respiration, heart-beat and endocrine secretions; but these activities may be modified by the thetan.

The human mind could be said to be the primary activity of the thetan with his own memory and ability plus the analytical standard memory banks, modified by the reactive memory banks of the genetic entity, and limited by the mechanical abilities and adaptabilities in action of the body itself.

These four parts of homo sapiens are detachable one from the other.

The personality and beingness which actually is the individual and is aware of being aware and is ordinarily and normally the "person" and who the individual thinks he is, is the thetan; and this awareness can continue, is clarified and is not interrupted by a detachment from the body which is accomplished by standard processing.

The thetan is immortal and is possessed of capabilities well in excess of those hitherto predicted for Man and the detachment accomplishes in the sober practice of science the realization of goals envisioned but questionably, if ever, obtained in spiritualism, mysticism and allied fields.

The anatomy of the beingness of Man is one of the lesser studies of Scientology where the beingness relates only to homo sapiens, for the detachment of the thetan by standard operating procedure is in common practice a simplicity, and it is therefore unrewarding to explore to much greater depths the remaining combination of the standard and reactive banks, the genetic entity and the body, since the last three are a specialized combination. Nevertheless the development of the technology necessary to bring about a complete state of beingness of that which a man actually is found to be, has provided considerable data and technology in the field of memory recordings, the peculiarities of energy behaviour around and about the body, the history of the evolutionary line, the identity of the genetic entity and much of the construction of the body itself, as well as the construction of the real universe. The bulk of the data which concerns homo sapiens, other than the beingness of the thetan, has been covered adequately earlier and elsewhere.*

* See Foreword

Footnote

In earlier efforts to better his state of beingness, Man has considered homo sapiens as an inseparable unit which was either alive or dead. Further, Man has thought it necessary, when he thought about it at all, to address and reduce the inroads of the past before the individual could assume any high level of beingness in the present. In Dianetics it was found that the mind was sub divisible into two parts, the first was the analytical mind which did the actual thinking and computing for the individual but which, in the present civilized state of Man, was almost submerged. The second was the reactive mind. The reactive mind was considered to be a stimulus-response mechanism which derived and acted upon the data of experience without thought. The content of the reactive mind was found to be the accumulated bad experiences of the organism not only in its current lifetime, but in the other lifetimes which it apparently had led in order to accomplish the task of evolution and to arrive at its present state of structural beingness. The reactive mind was the blueprint but it was also the stimulus-response dictator of action. The formula which described the reactive mind was that everything is identified with everything. Dianetics accomplished a great deal in the elevation of beingness by reducing the most violent incidents in the reactive mind by a process known as the erasure of engrams. An engram was a period of momentary or long pain and unconsciousness such as would occur in an injury, operation or illness. Such incidents could be reduced simply by "returning" the individual to the moment of the accident and then going over the accident step by step, perceptic by perceptic, as though it was happening again. After this had been done several times, the accident was found to have no more command value upon the individual. The reduction of the command value of the reactive mind was found to be necessary to a proper resolution of aberration. Understand that the reduction of the command value of the reactive mind was the goal, not merely the reduction of the reactive mind. When one is addressing the problems of an individual or group of men, the reduction of the command value of the reactive mind is still the goal where Scientology is used as a process to eradicate aberration. But two other methods are available for reducing this command value. The first of these lies in the removal of the analytical mind from proximity to the reactive mind and the increase then of the potential of the analytical mind until it can command and handle any reactive mind with ease. The second is simply the rehabilitation of the analytical mind by permitting it to use its creative ability in the construction of a universe of its own. It was found that there was no purpose in reducing incidents out of the reactive mind beyond the point where the analytical mind could step apart from the reactive mind, and then command it. Dianetics is a science which addresses itself directly to the reactive mind to reduce the command value of that reactive mind. Scientology is an embracive subject, much wider in application. It has as its goal the beingness that can exist without an energy or matter, which

The beingness of Man is essentially the beingness of theta itself acting in the mest and other universes in the accomplishment of the goals of theta and under the determination of a specific individual and particular personality for each being.

Scientology is the science of knowing how to know.

Scientology is the science of knowing sciences. It seeks to embrace the sciences and humanities as a clarification of knowledge itself.

One studies to know a science. His study is without avail when he does not know the science of study.

One lives and learns of life but life is not comprehensible to him, no matter how much he lives, unless he knows the science of life itself.

One studies the humanities. If he does not know how to study the humanities he often fails.

The physicist and the fission bomb expert know physics but not the humanities. They do not conceive the relationship and thus physics itself fails.

Into all these things—biology, physics, psychology and life itself—the skills of Scientology can bring order and simplification.

One lives better with Scientology since life, understood and controlled, becomes liveable.

---

is to say, without time, whether homo sapiens or not. Dianetics was an evolutionary step, a tool which had use in arriving at a higher level of knowledge; its use, however, produced slower results and much lower goals. Further, Dianetic processes were limited in that they could not be applied more than a few hundred hours without the reactive mind assuming a very high command level over the analytical mind due to the fact that the reactive mind was being validated continually in the process, whereas the better process was to validate the analytical mind. Medicine and psychology, as practised today, have absorbed and are using many of the principles of Dianetics without caring to be aware of the later developments in the field of the mind as represented here. Thus, the society absorbs and very often misunderstands knowledge.

A civilization could fare better with Scientology since that would not be pock-marked with unknowns and rendered null with chaos.

The only richness there is is understanding. That is all that Scientology has to give.

THETA-MEST THEORY

Scientology is essentially a study of statics and kinetics. If anything, it is more exact than what are called the physical sciences, for it is dealing with a theoretical static and a theoretical kinetic which are at the opposite ends of a spectrum of all motion.

One of the most valuable contributions of Scientology to knowledge is the definition of a true static. A static has no motion; it has no width, length, breadth, depth; it is not held in suspension by an equilibrium of forces; it does not have mass; it does not contain wavelengths; it has no situation in time or space. Formerly a static was defined only as a motionless object which definition is not adequate, since an object—or a state of rest for an object—is attained only by an equilibrium of forces and all objects have in themselves, if only on a molecular level, motion, and exist in space which is itself an integral portion of motion. Hence we see we are dealing with a higher level static.

The capabilities of the static are not limited.

The static interacts with the kinetic which is considered to be the ultimate of motion.

In Scientology, the static is represented by the mathematical symbol theta; the kinetic is called MEST.

Theta can be the property or beingness of any individual and is, for our purposes, considered to be individualistic for each individual.

MEST stands for matter, energy, space and time, and is a composite of the first letter of each. The word MEST appearing all by itself denotes the physical universe. MEST with a designation word after it designates another's universe.

The original of the Theta-MEST theory may be found in Science of Survival 1951. After the concept of the true static was reached, problems of processing began to solve much more rapidly, and the main proof of the Theta-MEST theory is its workability and the fact that it predicted an enormous amount of phenomena which, when looked for, were found to exist and which, when applied, resolved cases rapidly.

It is now considered that the origin of MEST lies with theta itself, and that MEST, as we know the physical universe, is a product of theta.

The physicist has adequately demonstrated that matter seems to be composed of energy which has become condensed in certain patterns. It can also be demonstrated adequately in Scientology that energy seems to be produced by and to emanate from theta. Thus it could be considered that theta producing energy, condenses the space in which the energy is contained, which then becomes matter. This theory of condensation is borne out by an examination of a state of aberration of many preclears who have been found to have descended down the tone-scale to the degree that their own space was contracted and who were found to be surrounded by ridges and who are thus "solid" to the degree that they are aberrated. Further, they can be found to be an effect in the ratio that they are so solidified. Further, a psychotic treats words and other symbols, including his own thoughts, as though they were objects.

Time

It is stated in the 1951 axioms that time could be considered to be the single arbitrary, and might thus be the single source of human aberration. A further investigation and inspection of time has demonstrated it to be the action of energy in space, and it has been found that the duration of an object roughly approximates its solidity.

Time could be considered to be a manifestation in space which is varied by objects. An object could be considered to be any unit manifestation of energy including matter.

It can be readily established that an individual loses his self-determinism in the ratio that he possesses objects and utilizes force.

Time could be considered to be an abstract term assigned to the behaviour of objects. It can be found to be regulatable by postulates.

The desire, enforcement and inhibition in the possession, giving and receiving of objects can be found to establish a time-track.

Time in the field of behaviour and experience becomes having. Having and Not Having form between themselves the interchanges which become survival.

If the auditor processes having, giving and receiving, energy and items, he will discover that he is processing time directly and has processed into a higher level the time sense and reaction of the preclear.

The primary manifestation of this is found in criminality, where the individual is unable to conceive the investment of energy to attain an object. He will not "work." The criminal in particular wishes to collapse and render without time, desiring and having; whereas this may be possible in one's own universe, it is not possible in the MEST universe. The MEST universe is so planned as to make work necessary in order to have, thus establishing a gradient scale of having. The criminal has not made the distinction between his own universe which he possibly once had and where he could attain things instantaneously, and the MEST universe. He thus has no "respect for property". The identification of his own universe with the MEST universe is so marked as to be in itself a highly aberrated identification, thus rendering his conduct destructive to himself and causing him to fail.

Space

Space is creatable by a thetan. He may also conserve, alter and destroy space.

Space is the first condition necessary to action. The second condition necessary is energy. The third condition is possession or not possession.

For the purposes of processing, and possibly for many other purposes, space can be considered to be the equivalent in experience of beingness. One is as alive as he has space and as he can alter and occupy that space.

The workable definition of space is "viewpoint of dimension": there is no space without viewpoint, there is no space without points to view. This definition of space remedies a very great lack in the field of physics, which defines space simply as that thing in which energy acts. Physics has defined space as change of motion or in terms of time and energy. Time has been defined in terms of space and energy; energy has been defined in terms of space and time only. These definitions, thus interdependent, made a circle out of which there was no exit unless one had a better definition for one of those items: time, space or energy. In such a way was the science of physics limited.

Space is the viewpoint of dimension. The position of the viewpoint can change, the position of the dimension points can change. A dimension point is any point in a space or at the boundaries of space. As a specialized case those points which demark the outermost boundaries of the space or its corners are called in Scientology anchor points. An anchor point is a specialized kind of dimension point. Any energy has as its basic particle a dimension point. The dimension point can be of different kinds and substances. It can combine in various ways, it can take on forms, become objects. It can flow as energy. A particle of admiration or a particle of force are alike dimension points. Dimension points, by shifting, can give the viewpoint the illusion of motion. The viewpoint, by shifting, can give the dimension points the illusion of motion. Motion is the manifestation of change of viewpoint of dimension points.

Viewpoints are not visible, but viewpoints can have dimension points which are themselves visible. The basic hidden influence is then a viewpoint. A material of the universe cannot exist in any universe without something in which to exist. The something in which it exists is space, and this is made by the attitude of a viewpoint which demarks an area with anchor points.

Rather than existing on theory, in common with other principles of Scientology this manifestation of created space can be experienced by an individual, who discovers that space can be made coincidentally with any other space. Space then, is not an arbitrary and absolute but it is creatable or uncreatable by a viewpoint.

Any being is a viewpoint, he is as much a being as he is able to assume viewpoints. Thus in any society we would inevitably have a statement of the infinity of viewpoint such as "God is everywhere." Beings instinctively assign the most beingness to that thing which would be everywhere and when Man desires to assign an unlimited power or command to anything he says that it is everywhere.

Energy

The basic unit of energy is the dimension point. A specialized kind of dimension point is the anchor point which demarks space, but this is again the basic unit of energy. Dimension points are created, controlled or uncreated by the thetan.

The qualities of energy are three in number: the first is its existing characteristics; the second is its wavelength; the third is its direction of flow or absence of direction of flow.

The characteristics can be divided into three classes in their turn. These are flows, dispersals and ridges. The flow is a transfer of energy from one point to another, and the energy in a flow can have any type of wave from the simplest sine-wave to the most complex noise-wave. Flowingness is simply the characteristic of transferringness. A dispersal is a series of outflows from a common point. A dispersal is, primarily, a number of flows extending from a common centre. The best example of a dispersal is an explosion. There is such a thing as an in-dispersal. This would be where the flows are all travelling toward a common centre. One might call this an implosion. Outflow and inflow from a common centre are classified alike under the word "dispersal" for handy classification. The third type of energy characteristic is the ridge. A ridge is essentially suspended energy in space. It comes about by flows, dispersals or ridges impinging against one another with a sufficient solidity to cause an enduring state of energy. A dispersal from the right and a dispersal from the left colliding in space with sufficient volume create a ridge which then exists after the flow itself has ceased. The duration of ridges is quite long.

Wavelength is the relative distance from node to node in any flow of energy. In the MEST universe, wavelength is commonly measured by centimeters or meters. The higher the frequency the shorter the wavelength is considered to be on the gradient scale of wavelengths. The lower the frequency the longer the wavelength is considered to be on a gradient scale. Radio, sound, light and other manifestations, each has its place on the gradient scale of wavelengths. Wavelength has no bearing upon wave characteristic, but applies to the flow or potential flow. A ridge has potential flow which, when released, may be supposed to have a wavelength. The various perceptions of the body and the thetan, each one is established by a position on the gradient scale of wavelengths. They are each one an energy flow.

Direction of flow, relative to the thetan, is of primary interest in energy study. There would be outflow and inflow. There could be outflow and inflow for a source point exterior to the thetan and caused by that source point, and there could be outflow and inflow by the thetan himself.

Matter

Matter is a condensation of energy. The more energy condenses, the less space it occupies and the greater its endurance becomes. A flow of energy has a brief duration. Flows of energy meeting and causing ridges obtain greater solidity and longer duration.

The solidification of matter is found to be itself duration or time. Energy becomes matter if condensed. Matter becomes energy if dispersed.

The manifestations of energy are essentially at long length the manifestations of matter; one cannot consider matter without also considering energy.

In processing, no differentiation is made between matter and energy beyond labelling the freer-flowing and more instantaneous forms "action" and the more solid and enduring forms "having."

In order to have matter, one must have space, must have had energy, and must *have*.

In order to have space, it is necessary to have a viewpoint and the potential in the viewpoint of creating anchor points. Thus, in order to view matter, much less control or create it, it is necessary to have a viewpoint.

AFFINITY, COMMUNICATION AND REALITY

In human experience, which is probably an experience senior to and creative of such a thing as the material universe, space, energy and matter become beingness, doingness and havingness.

Beingness is space regardless of energy and matter; doingness requires both space and matter; and havingness requires space and energy.

We have a gradient scale from space to matter which starts at the arbitrary number of 40·0 for our purposes and goes down to 0·0 for the purposes of homo sapiens and to $-8·0$ for the purposes of estimating a thetan. This gradient scale is called the tone scale.

Space is found to be a broad characteristic from top to bottom of the scale and necessary to each part of it, but it is discovered that one has less and less space the more the scale is descended. If one were to attain zero space for himself, he would attain, even as a thetan, zero. That the body has space and the thetan apparently, to himself, does not have space, is responsible mainly for the feeling of not-beingness on the part of the thetan which causes him to forget his own identity.

On this tone-scale, we have a theoretical point of no energy at 40·0, and a point where energy begins to be solid around 0·0; well below this level we have matter formed of the type known in the material universe. Thus one can see that this tone-scale is a gradient scale of energy, and that the energy is free toward the top of the scale and becomes less free and more fixed as one descends the scale.

A very important triangle in Scientology is the triangle called ARC. This stands for Affinity, Reality and Communication. It was used for some time before its relation to energy was understood.

Affinity is wave characteristic and is the range of human emotions. Human emotions manifest themselves in energy flows, dispersals and ridges. As the emotions drop down from high on the scale to low on the scale, they are found to follow a cycle of dispersals, flows and ridges. Each dispersal has a harmonic on the scale, each flow has a harmonic and each ridge has a harmonic. Looking up the scale from zero one finds death as a ridge and, in human emotion, an apathy. Apathy reaches up some extent from death but at this end the harmonics are very close together and there are two unnamed human emotions immediately above apathy. One of them, next above apathy, is a flow; immediately above that there is a fearlike dispersal. The next named emotion above apathy is grief. Grief is a ridge and is occasioned by loss. Immediately above grief there is a flow. The next named emotion, however, is the next level, the dispersal called fear which is a drawing away. There is a flow immediately above this called covert hostility. Above covert hostility is anger which is a solid ridge. Between anger at 1·5 and antagonism at 2·0 there is a dispersal—unnamed but visible in behaviour. At 2·0 we have the flow outgoing called antagonism. Above this at 2·5 there is an idle dispersal known as boredom. Above boredom at 3·0 is a ridge called conservatism. At 4·0 we have another flow called enthusiasm. Each one of these points is a harmonic of a lower point. The characteristic of energy whether a flow, dispersal or ridge, expresses itself in human emotion in terms of affinity. Affinity is the cohesiveness of human relationships, and can be acceptance or rejection of such relationships. Affinity as here used is a degree of emotion. Its equivalent in the MEST universe is the cohesion and adhesion or revulsion from matter and energy itself as found in positive and negative currents, and in forms of matter.

Communication is an interchange of energy from one beingness to another; in the thetan and in homo sapiens communication is known as perception. It is not solely talk, which is a symbolized form of communication which sums ideas which are themselves either a product of the tone-scale or are above the tone-scale as the case may be. Sight, of course, is at the wavelength of light. Sound is recorded as hearing. Tactile and smell are low-level wave types of the particle variety. And all other perceptions can be found on this gradient scale of wavelengths, modified by the wave characteristic in terms of type, whether sine or more complex. The auditor must realize that communication is essentially directed or received energy and is inhibited by the willingness or unwillingness of the preclear to take responsibility for energy or forms of energy. Where responsibility is low, perception is low.

Reality is established by wave direction or lack of motion. As one ascends the tone scale from 0·0 he finds the realities are strongest at the points of flow and are weakest at the points where there are ridges on the scale. The reality of apathy, grief and anger is very poor, but in the immediate vicinity of these there are more intense realities. Reality is established by agreement or disagreement or no opinion. Agreement is an inflow to the individual; disagreement is outflow from the individual; no opinion can be established by the proximity of the individual to the centre of a dispersal or by a ridge. Because of its wealth of energy and energy forms, the thetan finds himself ordinarily outdone in energy emanation by the Mest universe. Thus he is the target of an almost continuous inflow which causes him to have a consistent and continual agreement with the MEST universe. He seldom disagrees with the MEST universe, and the best processing one can do is to break this agreement and turn it into an opposite flow, for only in this wise can a preclear's ability to handle energy and be responsible for it be re-established. If you ask a preclear to get the concept of agreeing, he will find himself experiencing an inflow upon himself. Hypnotism is performed by causing a subject to receive a continuous rhythmic or monotonous flow from the operator. After this flow has continued the subject will accept any reality which the operator cares to deliver unto him. It is in this case, evidently, with the MEST universe, and the solidity of the MEST universe is completely dependent upon one's acceptance of it in terms of agreement. Reality in essence is agreement or disagreement. When one speaks of reality, he speaks in terms of the MEST universe. The MEST universe, according to any computation one cares to make upon it, is found to consist of a high-level agreement amongst us. Those who disagree with the MEST universe are punished by the MEST universe. From the standpoint of the MEST universe, the greatest reality would be had by matter itself and this seems to be its evident goal toward the thetan, to make him into solid energy. The reality on one's own universe is poor because he is in a comatose state of agreement with the MEST universe. It is found on processing, however, that a preclear is in poor condition in direct ratio that he has accepted and agrees and complies with the MEST universe, and is in good and active condition in direct ratio to the degree he can break this flow of agreement and establish his own flows and thus create his own universe. One's appreciation of the MEST universe is almost uniformly the energy which one himself places upon the MEST universe, in other words his illusions. When he loses his hopes and dreams (his illusions), it is because he has lost his ability to emanate energy back at the MEST universe and is dependent upon the energy the MEST universe thrusts at him.

ARC thus form a tone-scale. This tone-scale at any level finds a comparative state in affinity, in the reality and the communication abilities of the preclear. Thus, by testing the preclear and discovering his chronic emotion, his chronic state of agreement or disagreement, and his ability to communicate or not communicate, one establishes a level on this tone-scale. ARC form a triangle the corners of which are all at a single level. Thus if one wishes to create an increase of tone for the preclear—and one must do that to increase his self-determinism—he will find that he cannot raise the emotional state of the preclear without also addressing the reality and communication of the preclear. He cannot raise

23

the reality of the preclear without addressing his affinity and communication problems. He cannot raise communication with the preclear without addressing his reality and affinity problems. The worst mistake an auditor can make is to undervalue this triangle in processing. A more or less complete tone-scale can be found in *Science of Survival*, and Book I of that volume is devoted entirely to an evaluation of the tone-scale and people.

There are two positions on the tone-scale for the preclear when he is still a homo sapiens. The composite known as homo sapiens is considered to be dead at 0·0 and can rise on the tone-scale to slightly above 4·0. Thus homo sapiens has this as his range. The thetan, however, who, in homo sapiens, is below the level of awareness of self in terms of space and energy, has a wider range; and, as the thetan is basically the preclear and the beingness and identity of the preclear in actuality, this second range is even more important. This second range goes from −8·0 to 40·0 on the tone-scale. The optimum position for the thetan is considered to be 20·0 which is the point of optimum action. A homo sapiens as such could not attain this level of the tone-scale because of his physical limitations.

Identity Versus Individuality

The most common confusion on the part of a preclear is between himself as an identified object and his beingness. One's beingness depends upon the amount of space which he can create or command, not upon his identification or any label. Identity as we know it in the MEST universe is much the same as identification, which is the lowest form of thought. When one is an object and is himself an effect, he believes that his ability to be cause is dependent upon his having a specific and finite identity. This is an aberration; as his beingness increases his individuality increases, and he quickly rises above the level of necessity for identity for he is himself self-sufficient with his own identity.

The first question a preclear undergoing theta clearing asks himself is quite often: "How will I establish my identity if I have no body?" There are many remedies for this. The worst method of having an identity is having a body. As his individuality increases and his beingness expands—these two being almost synonymous—he is less and less concerned with this problem; that he is concerned with the problem tells the auditor where he is on the tone-scale.

One of the control mechanisms which has been used on thetans is that when they rise in potential they are led to believe themselves one with the universe. This is distinctly untrue. Thetans are individuals. They do not as they rise up the scale, merge with other individualities. They have the power of becoming anything they wish while still retaining their own individuality. They are first and foremost themselves. There is evidently no Nirvana. It is the feeling that one will merge and lose his own individuality that restrains the thetan from attempting to remedy his lot. His merging with the rest of the universe would be his becoming matter. This is the ultimate in cohesiveness and the ultimate in affinity, and is at the lowest point of the tone-scale. One declines into a brotherhood with the universe. When he goes up scale, he becomes more and more an individual capable of creating and maintaining his own universe. In this wise (leading people to believe they had no individuality above that of MEST) the MEST universe cut out all competition.

Beingness

Space is not necessary to the beingness of a thetan when the thetan is above the tone level of 40·0 and can create space at will. He creates space to have specific beingness. At 40·0 space and beingness can be considered to be interchangeable. Beingness can exist without any energy or matter, which is to say, without time.

However, in this universe, in order to achieve a state of beingness, which is more to our point here, it is necessary to have a viewpoint from which dimension points can be created or controlled. One has as much viewpoint as he has space in which to view in relationship to other viewpoints having space in which to view, thus one has a condition of relative beingness.

Doingness

Action requires space and energy manifestations, and the definition of action could be doingness directed toward havingness. In order to accomplish action, a preclear must be able to handle energy.

Doingness with energy and objects as found in the MEST universe is very far from the only method of producing existence. This is a specialized form of behaviour and may exist in any universe but is very peculiar to the MEST universe.

Havingness

Time is an abstract manifestation which has no existence beyond the idea of time occasioned by objects, where an object may be either energy or matter. Time can be defined as change in space, but where one attempts to define motion as change in space, the definition lacks usefulness since one does not define what is changing in space; there must be something there to change in space in order to have the illusion of time.

As was earlier discovered in Scientology, the single arbitrary is time. This is because time did not exist as such but stemmed from havingness. When Man experiences "time," he is experiencing havingness or not-havingness.

Time is summed up as "had," "have," and "will have." Goals in the MEST universe are summed uniformly under the heading of "will have." One engages in action in order to have.

This is one of the most important points of processing. The individual has made a postulate to have and has then gained something he did not want at every single point on the time track where you find him stuck. He desired to have a castle. He may have been engaging in an action which would gain for him a castle and was stopped and killed by an explosion which destroyed a wall before him. The explosion caught him with a postulate that he would have and gave him something he did not want. Struggling with the facsimile afterwards, the auditor will find that the incident began with the postulate to have and is now in a state of indecision since the explosion is unwanted.

Bluntly, any and all aberrative incidents to be discovered in a preclear are a reversal of havingness where the preclear did not want something and had to have it or wanted something and could not have it or wanted something and got something else.

The entire problem of the future is the problem of goals. The entire problem of goals is the problem of possession. The entire problem of possession is the problem of time.

Time is impossible without possession of objects.

Thus is resolved one of the weightier problems of the human mind. The auditor may find it difficult to encompass this principle, since time may continue to exist for him as an entity, an unknown and hovering thing. If he will use the principle that the past is had or did not have, that the present is has or does not have and that the future is will have or will not have, and that past, present and future are divided and established entirely by desire, enforcement and inhibition of havingness, he will find his preclear recovering swiftly.

Universes

A universe is defined as a "whole system of created things." There could be, and are, many universes, and there could be many kinds of universes: we are for our purposes here interested in two particular universes. The first of these is the Mest universe, that agreed upon reality of matter, energy, space and time which we use as anchor points and through which we communicate. The other is our personal universe which is no less a matter of energy and space.

These two universes are entirely distinct and it could be said that the principal confusion and aberration of the individual stems from his having confused one for the other. Where these two universes have crossed, in the mind of the individual, we find a confusion of control and ownership for the reason that the two universes do not behave alike.

Whereas each one of these universes was apparently founded on the same modus operandi as any other universe, which is to say, the creation of space by putting out anchor points, the formation of forms by combinations of dimension points, the Mest universe and one's own universe do not behave similarly *for him*.

One's own universe is amenable to instantaneous creation and destruction, by himself and without argument. He can create space and bring it into a "permanent status." He can create and combine forms in that space and cause those forms to go into motion and he can make that motion continuously automatic or he can regulate it sporadically or he can regulate it totally, and all by postulate. One's envisionment of one's own universe is intensely clear. The reality of one's own universe is sharper and brighter, if anything, than his reality on the Mest universe. We call one's attitude towards his own universe "actuality," and his attitude towards the Mest universe, since it is based upon agreement, "reality."

Unless an individual is at a very high operating level, he conceives it necessary to use physical force and to apply MEST universe forces to MEST universe forces in order to get action, motion and new forms. His activity in the MEST universe is an activity of handling energy and his ability to exist in the Mest universe is conditional upon his ability to use force. The MEST universe is essentially a force universe, a fact which is, incidentally, antipathetic to most thetans. One's ability to handle the MEST universe is conditional upon his not abdicating from his right to use force, right to give orders, his right to punish, his right to administer personal justice, and so forth. We are presented in the MEST universe with a crude and brutal scene wherein gigantic forces

28

are in pressure against gigantic forces and where the end of all seems but destruction. Paradoxically, in the MEST universe, destruction of form only is possible, since by the law of the conservation of energy, the destruction of actual material objects is impossible, only conversion being attainable.

In the MEST universe ethics seem to be a liability, honesty is all but impossible save when armed with force of vast magnitude. Only the strong can afford to be ethical, and yet the use of strength begets but the use of strength. In the MEST universe we are confronted with paradoxes upon paradoxes where behaviour is concerned, for behaviour in the MEST universe is regulated by stimulus-response and not by analytical thought or reason. The MEST universe demands of us complete and utter obedience and agreement on the penalty of extermination, yet when one has agreed entirely with the MEST universe he finds himself unable to perceive it with clarity.

In one's own universe, on the other hand, honesty, ethics, happiness, good behaviour, justice, all become possible.

It is one of the operations of the MEST universe that it is a jealous universe and those who are thoroughly imbued with the principles of the MEST universe have even as their best efforts the goal of eradicating one's own universe. A control operation begins early in the life of almost every man, whereby his imagination is condemned. His own universe is not imaginary, but it may be said to be so and if his imagination is condemned, then he loses his ability to garnish the hardness and brutality of the MEST universe with hopes and dreams. When he loses this he becomes a slave of the MEST universe, and as a slave he perishes. His road to immortality lies, then, in another direction than in the complete subservient agreement with the MEST universe and the handling and conversion of its forces. This is a matter which has been subjected continuously to test and it is intensely surprising to people to discover that the rehabilitation of their creative ability, their own space, their own images, rehabilitates as well their ability to confront the MEST universe with a strong and ethical face.

Creative processing, especially where it divorces all thought from thought of the MEST universe and follows out along a line of the rehabilitation of one's own universe without attention to the MEST universe, is one level of processing which produces magnificent results and which is a standby in any case, no matter how difficult.

On the other hand, the rehabilitation of the MEST universe itself, in the concept of the individual, accomplishes a very great deal in processing, and could be said to compare with the rehabilitation of one's own universe; but the rehabilitation of one's ability to perceive the MEST universe is dependent upon his ability to perceive present time and the rehabilitation of that ability. Dwelling upon the MEST universe past or its future is fruitless, thinking about the MEST universe, attempting to predict the MEST universe, planning to reorganize and handle the MEST universe, all defeat one's ability to handle the MEST universe. When he simply begins to perceive the MEST universe in present time and to examine that which he sees, with the idea that he can be what he sees, he loses all fear of the MEST universe.

There is a differentiation process in one's own universe, a differentiation process exclusively for the MEST universe and a differentiation process which pulls apart one's own universe and the MEST universe.

The first of these processes simply goes about reconstructing one's own universe with no attention to the MEST universe. The second causes the individual to contact the MEST universe present time and to observe that present time continuously. The third differentiates between the MEST universe and one's own universe and consists of "mocking-up" one's own universe duplicate of every MEST universe object he can perceive, and then actually comparing these one against the other.

Creating space and mocking-up items in it is the rehabilitation of one's own universe and is a primary process.

Differentiating between two similar objects in the MEST universe such as two books, two chairs, two spaces, with one's MEST eyesight, accomplishes much in being able to face and handle the MEST universe.

The mocking-up of MEST universe duplicates, which is to say constructing a universe parallel to the MEST universe, is the mechanism by which facsimiles (following) are made and this process brings under control the mechanisms which make facsimiles.

The original definition of Scientology 8–8008 was the attainment of infinity by the reduction of the apparent infinity and power of the MEST universe to a zero for himself, and the increase of the apparent zero of one's own universe to an infinity for oneself. This is an ideal and theoretical process, it is not necessarily attainable in actuality or reality but it very well may be. It can be seen that infinity stood upright makes the number eight: thus, Scientology 8–8008 is not just another number, but serves to fix into the mind of the individual a route by which he can rehabilitate himself, his abilities, his ethics and his goals.

Terminals

At every turn in the examination of the MEST universe we discover that it is a two-terminal universe. In the manufacture of electricity it is necessary to have two terminals. In order to have an opinion evaluated, it is necessary to have an opinion against which the first can be evaluated. A datum can be understood in the MEST universe only when it is compared to a datum of comparable magnitude. This is two terminals operating in terms of thought. Two MEST universe terminals which are similar, placed side by side will discharge to some degree against each other. This is observable in gravity as well as in electricity.

A primary difference between the MEST universe and one's own universe is that one's own universe is not a two-terminal universe necessarily. One can mock up in one's own universe two terminals which will discharge against each other, but he can also at will mock up two terminals which are identical which will not discharge against each other.

There are a number of processes which could include double terminals. One terminal made to face another terminal (in terms of mock-up) can be discharged one against the other in such a way as to relieve aberration connected with things similar to the terminal thus mocked up. However, these two terminals do not furnish a double terminal of a communication line. A communication line is more important than a communication point. Thus, if one wished to discharge anything, he would desire to discharge the communication line. The MEST universe is intensely dependent upon communication lines rather than communication terminals. One takes two pairs of such terminals then, and standing them in relationship to each other, discovers that he has now four terminals but these four terminals furnish only two lines. These two lines will discharge one against the other.

This, as a limited process, should not be continued very long. It is of greatest interest in rendering assistance after an accident where it is only necessary to mock up the accident twice, or indeed, to mock up something similar to an injured limb, to have the pain and discomfort and aberration discharged. Should one burn one's fingers, it is necessary only to mock up his fingers twice side by side and then twice again, making four mock ups with two communication lines, to have the pain in the finger subside. The mock-ups discharge at the same time as one's injured finger re-experiences the incident. This manifestation is the manifestation of the MEST universe, it is not a manifestation of one's own universe and if practised over a long period of time is essentially an agreement with the MEST universe, a thing which should be avoided; thus it is a limited process.

A terminal is, in essence, any point of no form or any form or dimension from which energy can flow or by which energy can be received. A viewpoint then, is a sort of terminal, but a terminal must have a particle in order to do automatic interchanges and one finds that a viewpoint can be affected by the MEST universe only when the viewpoint has identified itself with some MEST universe article, such as a body. The rehabilitation of the viewpoint's ability to be, or not be, at will is essential in order that a viewpoint be self-determined about what is affecting him and what is not affecting him. This depends, of course then, upon what a viewpoint identifies himself with and depends upon the ability of the viewpoint to unidentify himself rapidly.

Terminals are anywhere in the MEST universe and can be manufactured, of course, in one's own universe. The difference is that any bit of solid, even on the level of an electron in the MEST universe, is, willy-nilly, a terminal; it is affected in certain ways, whether it likes it or not. Any particle in any object or any flow of energy is in itself a terminal. A terminal can be affected by any other terminal or can affect, to some degree, other terminals.

This cross-relationship of terminals in the MEST universe is MEST universe communication. In one's own universe a flow is not necessary for the production of energy or potentials.

It is one of the sources of aberration that the scarcity of things in the MEST universe causes one to own only one of things; this is aberrative, since that one can gather into itself charges which are not discharged since there is nothing immediately similar to it. If one owned two of everything he had and if these two things were nearly identical, he would find that his worry and concern about these objects was greatly decreased. A child, for instance, should have two dolls alike, not simply one doll. The reason for this is that two terminals will discharge, one against the other. The thetan is capable of mocking himself up to be exactly like everything he sees. As a matter of fact, whatever a thetan can see, he can be. Thus, the thetan makes himself into a terminal for everything he sees whenever there is an absence of a duplicate. Thus the thetan is in the danger of having

33

everything in the MEST universe discharging against him the moment he alters his relationship to the MEST universe. This fixes him in the belief that he cannot alter his relationship to the MEST universe. Actually he is rather rapidly disabused of this conception by processing. It is rather interesting to "double-terminal" in mock-up form the childhood toys of an individual. He will find there is an enormous amount of charge simply in the fact that these toys were made out of MEST. The favourite doll has a gravitic influence upon him.

Completely aside from the terminals one finds in an electric motor and which produce so much current by reason of being separated by the base of the motor, the subject of terminals goes into behaviour and explains in a great measure behaviour on a stimulus-response basis in the MEST universe. Indeed, it could be said that the MEST universe came into being by one terminal demanding attention from another terminal and these two terminals thereafter facing each other continuing a discharge one to the other. With very aberrated people, one cannot long discuss things with them without getting the manifestation of terminals, for the very aberrated fix on a terminal easily.

It could be said that the MEST universe is the average of agreement amongst viewpoints and that the laws of the MEST universe, no matter how physical, are the result of this agreement; and, indeed, this definition suffices for those conditions which are supposed to be "reality." The MEST universe is very real, but any hypnotist can instruct a hypnotized subject into the construction of a universe which has tactile, sight, sound and any other manifestation possessed by the MEST universe, and who is to say then, that the hypnotized subject is not perceiving a universe? For one's own perception of the MEST universe consists of his placing an object in proximity to or against another object, and both of these objects are found to be objects of the MEST universe. This is overlooked by individuals when they, for instance, strike a desk with their fist. It is the favourite declaration of the materialist (that individual who is in a frantic state of insistence upon the existence of the MEST universe) that "this is real." The effects he is creating are being created by a hand that is made out of MEST on an object which is MEST. The individual has overlooked the fact that the hand with which he is doing the pounding is itself MEST and that his knowledge of that hand is actually no more than his perception of it. This is a problem in two terminals.

Behaviour of Universes

It could be said, then, that the difference between the microcosm (one's own universe) and the macrocosm (the MEST universe) is the difference between commanding it and agreeing about it. One's own universe is what he would construct for a universe without the opposition or the confusion of other viewpoints. The MEST universe is that upon which one agrees in order to continue in association with other viewpoints. This may very well be the sole difference between these two universes.

This is exemplified by one's behaviour-attitude in his own universe as compared with his behaviour-attitude in the MEST universe. In one's own universe, the individual expansively plans and devises (once he is fairly confident of it) along the lines of beauty and happiness. In the MEST universe, even when one has been rehabilitated to some degree, one's attitude still must consist of a certain amount of watchfulness and co-operation.

One's universe is an unthwarted sway, the MEST universe is a compromise. When one has compromised too long and too often, when he has been betrayed and ridiculed and is no longer able to create what he believes to be desirable, he descends down to lower levels and in those levels, he is still more compelled to face the MEST universe, and as such, loses much more of his ability to handle the MEST universe. When an individual's ability to create his own universe is rehabilitated it will be found, strangely enough, that his ability to handle the MEST universe has been rehabilitated. In fact, this is the most secure route as represented in 8–8008 as a road.

By actual experiment it can be demonstrated that one's ability to mock-up a universe of his own and the resulting improvement of his perceptions to that universe bring about an ability to perceive the MEST universe. Indeed, it might be inferred as something like a proof that the MEST universe in itself is an illusion based upon agreement in view of the fact that the rehabilitation of the ability to view illusion rehabilitates the ability to view the MEST universe.

Thought, Emotion and Effort

Thought is the highest level attainable. It is of two varieties; one is clear thought established by will which is from 10·0 up on the tone-scale, to well above 40·0; the other is thought established by counter-efforts as in homo sapiens and governed entirely on a stimulus-response basis. The first could be called self-determined thought; the second could be called reactive thought.

Self-determined thought expresses itself as will and consists of the making of postulates based on evaluations and conclusions. Will does not exist in time when it is at this level. Homo sapiens' will, as Schopenhauer once remarked, is stubbornness taking the place of the intellect. Will-power in homo sapiens is most ordinarily demon-circuit power. Free from the body and its ridges which themselves contain stimulus-response thought, the thetan can change his postulates by making new evaluations and conclusions, and can express his will directly. It is very difficult for a thetan inside the head and confronted by the stimulus-response ridges of the body, to do other than obey these stimulus-response flows in agreement with the MEST universe.

Ideas are invariably and inevitably senior to force and action, if those ideas stem from self-determined thought. Ideas born out of stimulus-response thought bear at times an almost indistinguishable similarity to self-determined ideas, but are occasioned by associative logic. In homo sapiens, it is quite common for the person to believe himself incapable of originality. This is because the MEST universe will brook no competitor. Operating on a highly self-determined plane, originality is a simple thing to attain. What is called will-power, then, could have two manifestations: the first would be actual self-determined thought; the second would be a result of an enforced or inhibited thought. When homo sapiens attempts to exercise his will-power, he normally brings into flow the ridges around the body and is nullified by them and is pressed into aberrated behaviour.

Ideas, when in the form of self-determined thought, exist above the level of 40·0 on the tone-scale and extend down into the action band.

Ideas of the stimulus-response variety are occasioned by experience as held and contained in facsimiles and are actually dictated to homo sapiens by circuits.

Postulate processing is that processing which addresses the postulates, evaluations and conclusions of the preclear at the level of self-determined thought, yet postulate processing has some value when addressed to stimulus-response ideas. Postulate processing is the primary and highest method of processing a thetan. With creative processing, it constitutes Scientology 8–8008.

Emotion, as known to homo sapiens, extends from slightly above 4·0 down to 0·0, and depends upon the wave characteristic.

Effort is an even lower level manifestation than emotion. Matter would be the lower effort band.

Facsimiles

The best description of facsimiles is to be found in *Electropsychometric Auditing*. A facsimile is an energy picture which can be reviewed again.

Facsimiles can disperse or flow when addressed by new

energy, either exterior to the thetan or from the thetan. Thus the environment can set a facsimile into action or the thetan can set it into action. Homo sapiens is most normally controlled by directing energy at his facsimiles and setting them into action so as to cause him to dramatize facsimiles and training patterns.

Facsimiles are normally found to be fixed in large number upon ridges.

A facsimile contains more than fifty easily identified perceptions. It also contains emotion and thought.

There are many methods of processing facsimiles.

Assist Processing

An "assist" is the processing given to a recently injured human being or thetan in order to relieve the stress of live energy which is holding the injury in suspension. The direct running-out of the energy contained in the recent facsimile is done by continually running through the incident as though it were just that moment happening to the preclear and recovering from it all his desire to have it and to not have it. And when this has been done to an extent where the energy is desensitized and the injury less painful, the preclear is led to handle it as energy, placing it in different places and times and reversing it and doing other things with it.

The assist is very important, as it can cause an injury to resolve or a person to recover in a fraction of the time which would otherwise be required and, in many cases, it may save the life of the individual and has done so many times in the past. The auditor must know facsimile processing primarily to run an assist and in order to know more about the anatomy of the human mind.

As noted earlier under Terminals, an assist can be rendered by mocking-up the injured part or the scene of injury as two terminals and holding or recreating these mock-ups until the injury abates. While doing this it will be noted particularly that the mock-ups are at first uncontrollable in most cases and then become much more easily controlled. The uncontrollable factor of the mock-ups is answered by this; whenever a pair of mock-ups or a single mock-up misbehaves, which is to say, acts without the specific command of the person getting the mock-up, the person doing the mock-up should simply abandon the pair or single mock-up and put into its place again one which is doing what he wants it to do; in other words, a disobedient mock-up or pair of mock-ups is either put away or moved to the right or left or forced into control, and in its place the individual simply puts a mock-up which is obedient to his control. An auditor should be careful on this point, for an individual getting mock-ups will strain and worry and eventually discover, he thinks, that it is impossible for him to control his mock-ups. Using effort to control one's mock-ups is of little avail; one simply creates them. Where mock-ups are absent, one will appear if the individual will simply keep putting the thought forward that it will appear. If he puts forward the thought often enough and long enough, he will get such a mock-up. Where he can get only one of a pair of mock-ups, if he will keep putting the second one in it will eventually appear. What one is facing in double terminalling here is so much charge on a single subject that the charge dissipates the mock-up before the mock-up can be adequately perceived. No matter how briefly, when an individual has said a mock-up will be there a mock-up has appeared; that it has disappeared promptly does not mean that he cannot put a second mock-up there. Particular attention should be given to this in assists because an assist is essentially dealing with an injured member or a scene which contains pain.

In double-terminalling assists it will be found that the preclear becomes ill or in pain in spite of how innocent he may feel it is to hold two terminals out in front of him. The remedy for this is simply to hold the two terminals(or replace them if they disappear or misbehave)until the illness or feeling has abated.

One can handle worries in this fashion. One simply puts

up one worry and then duplicates it facing itself out in front of him and the thought discharges against the thought until the worry and the emotion connected with the worry disappear. Thought, emotion, and effort can be dissipated by double-terminalling in this fashion. It is again remarked that this is a limited technique and should not be continued endlessly as an end in itself. Thirty or forty hours of double-terminalling is much more than enough. The route pointed out by Scientology 8-8008 is a better route than double-terminalling. Double-terminalling is relegated to the level of assist and changing one's state of mind. Double-terminalling doubt against doubt undermines and gets at the bottom of every circuit; thus, it, as a technique, should not be entirely neglected.

Cycle of Action

A cycle of action is dependent for its magnitude upon a cycle of havingness. Because it is a cycle of havingness and beingness and doingness, it is generally viewed as a cycle of time, but, as we have seen, time is an abstract term to describe havingness.

The beginning and ending of a cycle depends upon the state of havingness. A cycle starts with not-havingness, continues through increased havingness, continues then in changed havingness and ends with no-havingness. These conditions of havingness bring about an illusion of time. Where a person does not possess anything, he does not conceive himself to have any time. Thus earlier parts of the track are lost to an individual since he has no time in them, for he has no possession in them.

The most basic description of this should be in terms of havingness, but the cycle can also be stated more abstractly in terms as follows: creation, growth, conservation, decay and death or destruction. This would be the cycle of any object; it would also be the cycle of action as it pertained to an object in the MEST universe.

A cycle of action is not necessarily fixed for all universes.

It is common to the MEST universe. There is no reason why in some universe the cycle should not run from decayed havingness into growth, but in the MEST universe it never does, except through the point of not-havingness, death or destruction.

A cycle of action can also be stated in another way, and this in terms of energy action. Motion is characterized by only three conditions, and all motion is part of the gradient scale of these three conditions. These conditions are: start, change and stop. This compares to creation, alteration and destruction in terms of experience.

In the "last 76 trillion years" the preclear has lived through "spirals." These spirals were at first very long and then shortened each time until the present spiral for most is about 40,000 years as compared with the initial spiral of 100 million years. Thus one can also plot the magnitude of havingness of the individual for each one of these spirals. A spiral is not unlike a life. A life is lived in a cycle of action. A past life is generally obscured because one does not have the body of that life and conceives himself to have now another identity and is not connected to the last life by a havingness. He is, however, definitely connected to his last lives by the facsimiles of those lives which he now ignores.

Past havingness, present havingness and future havingness mark past beingness, present beingness and future beingness and also past action, present action and future action. The past, present and future are established by havingness, but havingness, doingness and beingness alike should be processed as intimately connected in this cycle of action.

The condition of the body itself and its position on the cycle of action as applied to the current life establishes to a large degree the preclear's attitude toward processing. He will react toward processing much in the manner dictated by the condition of the body and its position on the cycle. The body goes through the stages of creation, growth, conservation, decay and death.

A person in his middle years desires no change and may

be difficult to process for that reason, since the auditor is seeking to attain change. A person in the later cycle area will run only succumb material and will actually make an effort to succumb through processing. His incidents are commonly those of grief and loss since these are the manifestations of havingness in decay. He has no hopes of having before him and all of his havingness ordinarily no longer with him from the past.

The thetan going on the wider cycle of the spiral is discovered early on the spiral to be in a high state of creativeness, a little later to be intent upon a growth of havingness, a little later attempting to change to avoid conserving, a little later to be conserving, and then to be intent only on decay and dying, and finally upon death itself. The auditor should differentiate very sharply between the cycle of the spiral as applying to the thetan and the cycle of a lifetime. He may find a very young person who is yet on the later part of a spiral. The body of the young person is still in the state of growth and apparently the person's life should be hopeful of much having. Yet the behaviour of the person in general is directed almost uniformly towards succumbing. When the thetan is exteriorized from the body, he is found to be listless and certain of the approaching end. He believes that he will be finished entirely at the end of this spiral. He is not normally aware of the fact that he will have another spiral after this; or, if he is, he thinks it will be a shorter spiral—which it will be; but this can be remedied by postulate processing.

Related Experiences

There is a table of relationships which the auditor must have. These are divided into three general columns. Any one of the columns may be addressed first, but all three columns must be addressed on any subject. The vertical levels of the columns can be considered to be terms which are synonymous.

40·0	20·0	0·0
Start	Change	Stop
Space	Energy	Time
Beingness	Doingness	Havingness
Positive	Current	Negative
Creation	Alteration	Destruction
Conception	Living	Death
Differentiation	Association	Identification

ARC applies to each column or for any one of the above statements of experience.

All eight dynamics apply to each column and thus to any of the above statements of experience.

DIFFERENTIATION, ASSOCIATION AND IDENTIFICATION

A special condition of start, change and stop manifests itself in the very woof and warp of the MEST universe and can be plotted on the tone-scale.

Differentiation is at the top of the tone-scale and is a condition of the highest level of sanity and individuality. Association or similarity is a condition which exists from the upper to the very low range of the scale. And identification is at the bottom of the scale.

The condition of the preclear can be established readily by his ability to associate. He can, however, associate much too well. Association is the essence of logic. Logic is the gradient scale of relating facts one to another. As logic reaches the lower part of the scale, this relationship becomes finer and finer until at last identification is reached and thought could be expressed in terms of $A = A = A = A$.

An excellent rendition of this—although one not related workably to experience and which did not have with it a truly workable therapy—is to be found in general semantics in the book *Science and Sanity* by Alfred Korzybski. Insanity is the inability to associate or differentiate properly. Experience itself becomes ungovernable at the lowest depth of identity. The more fixed the identity of the person may be, the less the experience of which he is capable. Fame has at its end a completely fixed identification which is timeless, but which unfortunately is matter and which equally unfortunately, is inaction.

The widest possible differentiation exists at the moment of creation. At this moment, one is committed to a cycle of action which, as it continues, is less and less governable by himself and is more and more governed by his environment. As his degree of havingness increases, he is increasingly governed by what he has had and what he has, and this determines what he will have which, of course, is less freedom, less individuality and more havingness.

Association expresses itself in the preclear in terms of the way he thinks. When he reaches a low level of association, he supposes himself to be thinking connectedly, but is actually thinking in a completely disassociated fashion, for he identifies facts with other facts which should not be identified. The actions of a man about to die or in extreme fear are not sane. Identification brings as its manifestation a solidity to all things including thought. The auditor who processes a preclear very low on the tone-scale who is neurotic or psychotic will readily discover that thoughts are objects to this preclear and that time itself is a matter of enormous concern to the preclear in many cases. Thoughts and incidents and symbols are objects. This is commonly seen in the society in the matter of over-concern about words. A person who has sunk low enough on the tone-scale so that words have become objects and must be handled as such, and exist without any real relationship to ideas, will stop a flow of ideas by an outrage of his word sense which, if he is low on the tone-scale, is easily outraged.

Differentiation, association and identification belong, rightly, on the tone-scale, and can be processed as part of the scale above. But they are a close gauge of thought itself and of ideas. An adequate tone-scale can be drawn for any individual using only the above three words.

The auditor will very often find an individual who is intensely logical and quite brilliant who is yet very difficult to process. This person has agreed with the MEST universe to such a degree that his association has assumed the proportions of near-solidity; the facsimiles and ridges of this individual have become much too solid and are consequently quite difficult to process. This condition of solidity may refer only to the body of the preclear which itself is old, and it may be found that the thetan—the preclear himself—is quite vital and capable of wide differentiation, but that this differentiation is being grossly limited by the ridges and

45

facsimiles which surround the body. Such bodies have a heavy appearance. It requires an enormously powerful thetan to handle them in spite of the solidity of the ridges surrounding the body.

Mathematics could be said to be the abstract art of symbolizing associations. Mathematics pretends to deal in equalities but equalities themselves do not exist in the MEST universe, and can exist only conceptually in any universe. Mathematics are a general method of bringing to the fore associations which might not be perceived readily without their use. The human mind is a servo-mechanism to all mathematics. Mathematics can abstractly form by their mechanics coincidences and differences outside the field of experience in any universe and are enormously useful. They can best be used when considered to be a shorthand of experience and in the light that they can symbolize what is beyond actuality. The essence of mathematics lies in differentiation, association, identification, which is to say, equalities must not be viewed as fixed in the real universe. Absolutes are unobtainable in experience but may be symbolized by mathematics.

Logic

Logic is a gradient scale of association of facts of greater or lesser similarity made to resolve some problem of the past, present or future, but mainly to resolve and predict the future. Logic is the combination of factors into an answer. The mission of the analytical mind when it thinks, is to observe and predict by the observation of results. Easily the best way to do this is to be the objects one is observing: thus, one can know their condition completely. However, if one is not sufficiently up the scale to be these objects it is necessary to assume what they are. This assumption of what they are, the postulating of a symbol to represent the objects and the combination of these symbols when evaluated against past experience or "known law," bring about logic.

The genesis of logic may be said to be an interchange of two viewpoints, via other dimension points by which one of the viewpoints holds the attention (one of the most valuable commodities in the universe) of the other viewpoint by being "logical" about why that viewpoint should continue to look. The basis of logic is "it is bad over there" or "there is a hidden influence which you cannot estimate but which we will try to estimate," "therefore, you should continue to look towards me." At its best, logic is rationalism, for all logic is based upon the somewhat idiotic circumstance that a being that is immortal is trying to survive. Survival is a condition susceptible to non-survival. If one is "surviving," one is at the same moment admitting that one can cease to survive, otherwise one would never strive to survive. An immortal being striving to survive presents immediately a paradox. An immortal being must be persuaded that he can not survive or that he is not or might become not, before he would pay any attention to logic. By logic, he can then estimate the future. Probably the only reason he would want to estimate the MEST universe, aside from amusement, is to keep alive in it, or to maintain something in a state of life in it. Logic and survival are intimate, but it must be remembered that if one is worried about his own survival and is striving for his own survival, he is striving for the survival of an immortal being. Bodies are transient, but bodies are an illusion. One could bring himself up the tone-scale to a point where he could create an imperishable body with ease.

It is interesting that those people who are the most logical are those people who in processing have to know before they are. When they are sent somewhere, they want to know what is there before they get there. There would be no point in going there if they knew, and if everyone knew what was there before they went there. Yet they will attempt to predict what is going to happen there and what is there by knowing. This knowingness is in terms of data and should not be confused with knowingness in terms of actual beingness. Logic is the use of data to produce knowingness; as such it is very junior to knowing something by being it.

If you were to double-terminal an individual who is customarily very logical, his body facing his body in terms of mock-up and each of the terminals being very logical, a surprising violence of interchange would take place. This is because logic is mainly aberration. The work which lies before you is a discussion of beingness and is the track of agreement which became evidently the MEST universe. Therefore this work appears to be logical but it appears also to be the central thread of logic. Apparently, these conclusions were reached by logic; they were not, they were reached by observation and by induction. That when tested they proved themselves in terms of behaviour demonstrates not that they are logical,but that they are, at least to a large extent, a discussion of beingness. Scientific logic and mathematical logic have the frailty of trying to find out what is there before one goes there. One cannot ever be, if he has to know a datum about the beingness first. If one is afraid to be, one will become, of course,logical. This is no effort to be abusive upon the subject of logic or mathematics, it is only necessary at this point to indicate a certain difference between what lies before you and a logical arrangement of assumption.

Patterns of Energy

Energy forms into many patterns. The geometry of this formation would make an intensely interesting study. The patterns, however, are formed by postulates and have no other existence.

The patterns of energy are viewed by the thetan in terms of pressors, tractors, explosions, implosions, pressor ridges, tractor ridges, pressor-tractor ridges, and balls and sheets.

The pressor is a beam which can be put out by a thetan which acts as a stick and with which one can thrust oneself away or thrust things away. The pressor beam can be lengthened and, in lengthening, pushes away.

A tractor beam is put out by a thetan in order to pull things toward him. The tractor beam is an energy flow which the thetan shortens. If one placed a flashlight beam upon a wall and then, by manipulating the beam, brought the wall closer to him by it, he would have the action of a tractor beam. Tractor beams are used to extract perceptions from a body by a thetan. Pressor beams are used to direct action. Tractors and pressors commonly exist together, with the tractor as a loop outside the pressor. The two together stabilize one another.

An explosion is an outflow of energy usually violent but not necessarily so, from a more or less common source point.

An implosion could be likened to the collapse of a field of energy such as a sphere toward a common centre point, making an inflow. It can happen with the same violence as an explosion, but does not necessarily do so.

A pressor ridge would be that ridge formed by two or more pressor beams operating against each other in conflict.

A tractor ridge would be that ridge formed by two tractor beams in conflict operating against each other.

A pressor-tractor ridge would be a combination of pressor-tractor flows in sufficient collisions as to form a solidification of energy.

A ridge is a solid body of energy caused by various flows and dispersals which has a duration longer than the duration of flow. Any piece of matter could be considered to be a ridge in its last stage. Ridges, however, exist in suspension around a person and are the foundation upon which facsimiles are built.

Two explosions operating against each other may form a ridge.

Two implosions operating away from each other may form a ridge. An explosion and an implosion operating together—or many explosions and implosions operating together—may form a ridge.

These manifestations of energy are used in handling energy, either in processing or in action.

Black and White

Black and white are the two extreme manifestations of perception on the part of the preclear.

The thetan perceives best his own energy, but when he perceives energy he desires to perceive it in white or in colour. Colour is a breakdown of whiteness. Seeing whiteness or colour, the thetan is able to discern and differentiate between objects, actions and spatial dimensions.

Energy can also manifest itself as blackness. A space containing black energy would be black, but a black space may be a space existing only without energy in it. This point of identification is quite aberrative, and drills to permit the thetan to handle blackness are mandatory in processing. If one remembers one's fear of blackness when a child, and that evil is represented as blackness, one will see the necessity for doing this. Blackness is the unknown, for it may contain energy or it may be empty or may be black energy.

Black energy flows are common on the tone-scale of wavelengths. There is, for instance, what is known as the black band of sound.

Some thetans will not perceive anything at all because they conceive themselves to be surrounded by blackness and are not sure whether the blackness has substance or is simply empty, and they have a timidity to discover which. Such a case is resolved by making the case drill with blackness until blackness can be turned on and off and located in time and space. Although this is briefly mentioned, it is a point of the largest importance.

Black and white running and black and white aesthetic running were old processes which are not necessarily vital today to processing. However, white energy runs easily, and where the preclear has a black spot of energy somewhere on an organ or somewhere in the environment of the body, the auditor asks him to turn it white in order to let it flow away. It may not flow away if it is black, either because it does not belong to the preclear (in which case he would see it as black) or because it is simply a spot of space with which he is not familiar. By turning it white he is able to handle it for he now knows it to be filled with his own energy.

One can run own determinism, other determinism, as concepts. In this case the preclear runs the one as long as he gets an area white and then runs the other to continue its whiteness. In such a way all the energy in the area is drained away.

The most common manifestation of a ridge is to have one side of a ridge white and the other side black. This is because the preclear conceives one side of it to have on it his own energy and the other side to have on it energy belonging to another. By running the concept that it is his own and then running the concept that it is another's, one runs both sides of a ridge, if he is running ridges.

Although live energy is generally conceived to be white, it can also be black. In running a preclear with an E-meter, it will be discovered as long as a flow is white and as long as a flow is running, that the needle will gradually rise. When a point of blackness appears in the field, the needle will halt and either will not rise again or will flick as the preclear gets a somatic. This flick is characteristic of the somatic. The stuck needls is characteristic of a black field. The auditor can sit watching a needle and be able to tell the preclear whenever the preclear has had a black area appear in the field. It is notable that somatics only occur in the presence of a black patch. This means that the unknown characteristic of the blackness is something the preclear has been holding away from him so as not to have it or that black wave energy is that energy used to impress pain. The latter case is the more probable although a great deal of work must be done upon this to establish beyond doubt the manifestation of blackness.

A preclear who cannot see colour in his facsimiles, cannot see it because he is unable to use energy with which to perceive. He will see things in terms of blackness or whiteness. He may be able to get black and white or he may be able to get only blackness. In the latter case he finds blackness in some way profitable and desirable; and running the concept of havingness, will have and have had blackness, and using drills in handling blackness—moving it from space to space in the environment and moving it into yesterday and tomorrow—will bring about control of blackness on the part of the preclear .

Perception

The entire subject of perception is the subject of energy. As the preclear goes down the tone-scale, he is less capable of differentiation and is thus less and less capable of handling energy and is more and more subject to energy, until at last he will not emanate or handle energy. Even in the higher ranges of this descent his perception begins to diminish.

The rehabilitation of perception is essentially the rehabilitation of force. Force is rehabilitated by rehabilitating the control of energy. This is done by ARC processing and in many other ways. The chief way in which this is done is by establishing the preclear's ability, by creative processing, to handle blackness.

An entire science called perceptics can easily be constructed and is mentioned in the original thesis (1948).

The rehabilitation of sight in the blind, hearing in the deaf, the ability to speak, anaesthesia of the body or body areas or the genital organs, depends upon the rehabilitation of the preclear's ability to handle energy. Creative processing, with particular attention to handling blackness, is essential in this process.

Force

In the axioms, force is defined as random effort. Effort is defined as directed force.

Force is essentially measured effort. It is quite common for individuals to be so protesting at what the MEST universe is doing that they abandon any and all force and, if asked to reassume force or use it, suppose that one is asking them to condone and assume punishment and destruction since these in the MEST universe are done with heavy quantities of force. There is, however, a gradient scale of force, for any energy manifestation may be called force. Even matter contains force.

For the purposes of processing, in order to avoid upsetting the preclear, who usually has very bad connotations with the word force, the auditor stresses instead the "handling of energy."

The use of energy would encompass any activity having to do with energy or matter.

Responsibility

The responsibility level of the preclear depends upon his willingness or unwillingness to handle energy. That preclear who is protesting against energy in any direction is abandoning responsibility in greater or lesser degree.

One obtains randomity (see Axioms) by abandoning responsibility in some sphere. He will then find himself in conflict in that sphere.

The gradient scale of responsibility is as follows: at 40·0 responsibility manifests itself as will and can be so pervasive that there is no randomity. This would be full responsibility.

At 4·0 responsibility would manifest itself in terms of action where roughly half one's environment or space had been selected for randomity and for which one would take no responsibility. At 20·0 responsibility would be 50 per cent of the total energy existing.

At 4·0 we find homo sapiens in his narrow environment disagreeing by using the emotion of enthusiasm with an existing state of affairs and directing energy toward the righting of that state of affairs. Even so, responsibility is low at this level.

At 2·0 blame enters the tone-scale as a major factor. This is the level of the tone-scale where fault is envisioned for the first time. Above this level there is sufficient breadth of understanding to see that interdependencies and randomities can exist without fault and blame. At 2·0, with the emotion of antagonism, an individual is assigning blame for lack of responsibility rather than trying to enforce responsibility.

At 1·5 blaming is almost the sole activity of the individual, and, while taking no real responsibility himself, yet he blames all on his environment and does so with violence.

At 1·1 one pretends to take some responsibility in order to demonstrate that others are at fault but one has no real responsibility.

At 0·9 or around the level of fear, one does not think in terms of responsibility but is willing to accept all blame in an effort to escape all punishment.

At 0·75, grief, the individual blames himself, and accepts the fault for what has occurred.

At 0·375, apathy, there is no question of either blame or responsibility. At this level one has become MEST.

On the tone-scale in *Science of Survival* one will find what might be expected to happen to materiel and communication and persons in the vicinity of those below 2·0 on the tone-scale. This stems normally from responsibility, or rather, its lack.

The keynote of responsibility is the willingness to handle energy. The rehabilitation of the thetan in the handling of energy brings about a rise in responsibility. If a person is low on the tone-scale and still exhibits responsibility, then his energy activity initially must be enormous for any segment of responsibility to exist low on the scale.

The processing of responsibility is one of the most vital processes. If one processes responsibility itself, he can expect sooner or later a theta clear. He would process it by brackets.

There is a condition known as the "glee of insanity." This is essentially a specialized case of irresponsibility. A thetan who cannot be killed and yet can be punished, has only one answer to those punishing him, and that is to demonstrate to them that he is no longer capable of force or action and is no longer responsible. He therefore states that he is insane, and acts insane and demonstrates that he cannot possibly harm them as he lacks any further rationality. This is the root and basis of insanity. Insanity is the only escape possible besides death.

Death has the value of convincing others that one can no longer be punished or feel. As long as one has a body, which can die, there is a limit to the amount he can be hurt. When there is no body, and there is no limit to the amount he can be hurt, his only answer is this plea of complete irresponsibility which is the "glee of insanity." This is found as an actual energy manifestation in the vicinity of sanitoria and can be felt as an emanation from the insane.

If the preclear is unable to conceive of "being happy about being insane" (which he usually cannot), get him to get the feeling of anticipation for a vacation. This is irresponsibility in one sense and in actuality, when deepened, becomes the "glee of insanity."

Happiness is the overcoming of not insurmountable obstacles toward the known goal of havingness. Stepping away from this track, feeling that one's work is too hard, these are forsakings of responsibility. A common method employed by low-toned people to reduce the power and ability of an individual and so place him under control is to convince him that he is tired and overworked. If they can so convince him, they can then get him to take a vacation. An examination of an individual who has been subjected to this will show that he was happiest when he was working and that before he "needed a vacation" many people worked on him to convince him that he should not work so hard, and thus turned what was actually play to him into work. Society almost demands that a man consider whatever he is doing as work and demands that he consider work as an unhappy thing. In looking around the society at those who gain easily, one finds only people who take a great deal of joy in working and who never think in terms of a vacation.

To run the bracket on responsibility, one would run the desire on the part of the preclear to be responsible, his desire not to be responsible, times when he has been forced to be responsible, times when he has been forced not to be responsible, times when he has been restrained from being responsible, times when he has been restrained from being not-responsible, times when he has been sympathized with because of his responsibilities and then all this as a bracket, the preclear doing it to others and others doing it to others. This run round and round as brackets produces marked results.

The joy of responsibility and the joy of irresponsibility should also be run in terms of brackets.

This becomes most effective when run in terms of responsibilities of having, the irresponsibilities of having, the responsibilities and irresponsibilities of having had, and of will have.

Before this has been run very long on some individuals, the glee of insanity will manifest itself and it must be very thoroughly run out. It is often a hectic, uncontrolled laughter. This should not be confused with line-charge laughter to which it is a cousin; a preclear who starts laughing over the serious things of his past is breaking locks, and can be made to laugh in this fashion for many hours if the chain reaction is started. The laughter which accompanies the "glee of insanity" has no mirth in it whatever.

Peculiar to this is what might be called the attitude of MEST. MEST is not responsible for anything. That preclear who has as his goal complete irresponsibility has also as his goal being complete MEST.

MEST has no space of its own, it causes no action except when acted upon, and it owns nothing but is itself owned.

Slaves are made by giving them freedom from responsibility.

The thetan high on the scale can make space or own space, has wide choices of action, and can create, change or destroy anything he wishes.

The Chart of Attitudes

In order to do rising-scale processing (as covered later), the auditor should know very well his Chart of Attitudes and the reasons underlying each column.

Survives	Right	Fully responsible	Owns All
Dead	Wrong	No responsibility	Owns nothing
Everyone	Always	Motion source	Truth
Nobody	Never	Stopped	Hallucination
Faith	I know	Cause	I am
Distrust	I know not	Full effect	I am not
Win	Start	Difference	Being
Lose	Stop	Identification	Had

This chart on the upper line in each of the above represents from 27·0 to 40·0. The lower line under each one represents 0·0.

Each one of these is a gradient scale with many intermediate points. In rising-scale running, one seeks the attitude of the preclear nearest to the lowest end of this scale and asks him to do a rising-scale to see how high he can change his postulate toward the upper end of the scale.

The last line is, of course, a repeat without the intermediate position of the earlier interdependencies of experience.

Survival

One of the first principles in the MEST universe, and that principle which, when discovered, resolved the problems of the mind, is the lowest common denominator of all MEST universe existence; the goal of life in the MEST universe is survival and only survival.

Survival equates behaviour in homo sapiens or in any life form. It also covers the wide field of ethics. The principle of survival was never intended to embrace theta itself for this has, of course, immortality and does not even necessarily move in MEST time.

Survival is nothing if not dependent upon havingness, action and beingness. It is most ordinarily viewed as the attempt in a life form to persist in a state of existence as long as possible.

Right-Wrong

Rightness is conceived to be survival. Any action which assists survival along the maximal number of dynamics is considered to be a right action. Any action which is destructive along the maximal number of dynamics is considered to be wrong. Theoretically, how right can one be? Immortal! How wrong can one be? Dead!

After a certain point on the tone-scale is reached by the preclear, he will tend instinctively to seek out and do right actions, but ordinarily homo sapiens is thoroughly engrossed in being wrong. Social politeness, with its violation of the Code of Honour, is quite non-survival. It might also be said, How wrong can one be? Human!

The accident prone and no-responsibility case in general is so intent on being wrong that he is incapable of conceiving right.

All jurisprudence is built upon the principle that sanity is the ability to differentiate right from wrong. Jurisprudence does not, however, give a definition of either rightness or wrongness. Thus, for the first time with this principle, rules of evidence and other matters in law can be established with some accuracy.

Absolute rightness, like absolute wrongness, is unobtainable. Rightness and wrongness are alike relative states.

Responsibility

(See text above.)

Ownership

In view of the fact that time can be conceived to be hav-ingness and in view of the fact that time itself is one of the most puzzling concepts which homo sapiens has ever sought to master, the whole question of ownership is subject to grave error, particularly on the part of homo sapiens.

Discussions in the above text demonstrate that individu-ality depends upon high-tone level and freedom, whereas identity, as such, would be at a complete level of reduction, a condition analogous to MEST.

It has long been recognized that "a rich man may as well try to get into Heaven as a camel through the eye of a needle." The auditor will suddenly discover this truth when he tries to process many rich and successful men. These have carried ownership to such an extent that they are themselves thoroughly encased in energy which is solidifying into MEST itself. Instead of having things, they themselves are had by things. Their freedom in motion is enormously reduced, although they have tricked themselves into believing that possession will increase that freedom.

The auditor will find his preclear upset nowhere on the tone-scale as he will on the subject of ownership. A child-hood, for instance, is intensely upset by the subject of owner-ship since the child is given to understand that he owns certain things and is then commanded in every action he takes with those items. A child cannot have possession, free and clear, of anything in the average family. He is given shoes and is told to take care of them and is punished if he does not take care of them although he apparently owns them. He is given toys and is harassed whenever he abuses them. He finally becomes convinced that he owns nothing and yet he is in a state of anxiety about owning things. Therefore he will try to possess many things and will completely overestimate or underestimate the value of what he has. The auditing of childhood ownership is a fruitful field for the auditor.

That preclear who is upset on the subject of time, even faintly, is, and has been, enormously upset on the subject of ownership, since havingness and its manifestations are themselves the MEST universe trick of giving us an illusion of time.

Everyone-Nobody

(See material above on Identity versus Individuality.)

It may be confusing to the preclear that being everybody can be conceived at both ends of the tone-scale. The difference is that at the bottom end of the scale, the preclear is making the mistake of considering the "somebodies" around him as MEST. He can be their MEST identities. At the top of the scale, while still retaining his own identity, he can be anyone's identity but this is on a theta level and is disassociated from MEST. That preclear who goes around believing he is other people is usually at the bottom end of the tone scale and has confused his own body with the bodies he sees because he does not have a proper view of his own body and so can easily mistake it for the bodies of others.

When an individual is low on the tone-scale, he easily does a life continuum for others because he himself is so encased in MEST and so poorly recognizes his own identity that he can conceive himself to be anyone without knowing what he has done.

The question of valences and life continuums is difficult to resolve in direct ratio that the preclear conceives himself to be MEST.

MEST, lacking the ability to create space and to produce directive action is, of course, nobody. When a man is convinced he is a nobody he has been convinced at the same time that he is MEST.

Always-Never

We have already seen that objects give us the illusion of time. The ability to create objects is interchangeable with the ability to have an actual forever.

There would be an illusory forever which would be dependent upon the duration of an object and its apparent solidity. One might also say that the MEST universe seeks to own one by pretending that immortality is something difficult to buy and is only purchased by achieving an identity or being an object. The ultimate in this is, of course, being a part of the MEST universe. One might say jocularly that every planet in the MEST universe was once one or more people. A considerable reaction can be got from a preclear by making him conceive a feeling of devotion toward the "older" gods who were here and who built this universe and who have left it to him. Deeply religious feelings are very often based upon this idea. Some astonishing reactions can occur in a preclear when running this concept.

The real way to be assured of a great deal of time is to be able, of course, to create time, and this would be to a thetan the true concept of always. Time is created, at least in this universe, by creating energy and objects, and by being able to make the universe agree with oneself, not by having the universe continually making one agree with it.

Motion Source-Stopped

The ability to cause motion is dependent, whether the individual realizes it or not, upon the ability to conceive space. Creation of space is the first requisite for the creation of motion.

When one can no longer create space and cannot conceive any space to be his own, he can be considered to be stopped. That individual who is tremendously concerned with being stopped is losing his ability to create space. When he is no longer able to create space, he is himself MEST.

Somebody once said that it was a poor man who was not king in some corner. One might add to this that one is not only poor but he does not exist when he cannot create a corner. One could obtain a very amusing viewpoint of this by watching the conduct of a dog who, theta-motivated like every life form, is bravest in his own front yard; and even a mastiff proceeds with some caution when in the front yard of a pekinese. This is a case of ownership of space and, in some slight degree, the ability to create a space to own.

One processes this by moving mock-ups into an auto created space.

Truth-Hallucination

The highest one can attain to truth is to attain to his own illusions. The lowest one can descend from truth is a complete acceptance of MEST universe reality, for this below a certain level becomes scrambled and brings on the condition known as hallucination. Hallucination is not self-generated; it comes about only when a person is an effect to such an extent that he is almost dead.

What is commonly believed to be truth is agreement upon natural law. This would be the truth of the MEST universe which would be the lowest common denominator of agreement upon any one subject. Where the MEST universe is concerned, acceptance of such truths is dangerous.

In Scientology one is studying the lowest common denominators of agreement which bring about an acceptance of the MEST universe and prohibit the creation of one's own universe, which latter ability alone makes possible perception of the MEST universe which is itself an agreed-upon illusion.

Truth in Scientology is the study of the lowest common denominator of agreement, plus the establishment of the true ability of the thetan. The true ability of the thetan is a truth much higher than the truth of the MEST universe itself and, if it has ever before been known, the difficulties of communicating it have been such as to inhibit its promulgation.

It can be seen there is truth above what passes for "truth" in the MEST universe. Scientific truths gained from deductive observations of behaviour of the MEST universe are themselves manifestations of agreements on the part of beings —thetans—who are capable of much wider creation and agreement than that represented in the MEST universe.

We have answered in Scientology a good portion of "what is truth?"

Faith-Distrust

There is no more over-rated quality in existence than faith.

The subject who, under the hands of a hypnotist operator, conceives an enormous agreement with the hypnotist, is experiencing faith as it is commonly understood. In this state the subject can perceive anything which the hypnotist may direct.

In order to understand faith, one must be able to differentiate between *faith-in* and faith. The difference between these two conditions is a direction of flow which earlier we found to be reality itself. Faith-in is an inflow of agreement and the placing of one's beingness and doingness under the control of another, and is, in other words, the sacrifice of one's universe. This is the basic mechanism wherein, all along the whole track, thetans have been recruited in some cause or mystery, and have surrendered to this their own identity and ability. A little of this goes a very long distance. It is in essence the basic trick of hypnotism and by it one can convert and reduce the abilities of a subject for any purpose.

Faith-in is an inflow and brings about the acceptance of reality other than one's own. Faith itself would be without flow where one was in a full state of beingness and, with this condition, one could occasion faith itself to occur within his own universe, or could occasion people to have faith in him.

The auditor will find one of the more aberrative phases of the preclear in his failure to obtain from others faith in himself,and his acquiescence to their demands on any dynamic that he have faith in them.

Because it is entirely true that a being lacking in faith is low in tone, the fact can be traded upon with great ease.

Distrust is not the lowest end of the scale, but begins to set in as a neurotic or psychotic condition at about 1·5. Actually faith interchanges with distrust in gradient levels all the way down the tone-scale and they alternate one with the other as one goes deeper and deeper into the MEST universe. The lowest level of this scale is not distrust but complete faith-in, which is the condition held by MEST which is supine to any sculptor.

This column might also be called the column of belief-disbelief or the column of reality-unreality. The auditor can expect the preclear as he rises up the tone-scale to pass through the various shades of distrust and the various shades of faith. This is often quite upsetting to the preclear for he cannot conceive himself to be rising in tone.

It is very noteworthy that a preclear, when low in tone at the beginning, will pass inevitably through various strata of revulsion for the MEST universe and then for his own universe. The revulsion he can conceive for the MEST universe objects and for being in the MEST universe can become unthinkably distressing to him. When this condition has occurred, the auditor can be reassured by the fact that the preclear is rising in scale but has hit upon one of the levels of this column, and that a higher level and a more comfortable one immediately succeeds as processing is continued. This is simply a problem of reversing directions of flow. If the auditor is running flows he will find that an in-flow is shortly succeeded by an out-flow and this out-flow is shortly succeeded by another in-flow. These are in essence agreements and disagreements alternating one after the other and each one is slightly higher on the tone-scale than the last.

I Know—I Know Not

Epistemology has long been the senior study of philosophy; Scientology is itself the science of knowing how to know.

The study of knowledge is in essence, in the MEST universe, a study of data. Data in the MEST universe are usually recorded in facsimiles. Thus one can go in two directions toward knowledge. The first is knowing what one is, and the second is knowing what has happened to one in the MEST universe and searching for identity in the MEST universe.

There is no more tragic track than the sordid ransacking of facsimiles to discover TRUTH for all one discovers is what is true for the MEST universe. This wandering and endless trail is bleak with the bones of lost beingness. Earlier explorers have, almost without exception, destroyed themselves in this search for TRUTH in the MEST universe, for all they discovered was further and further agreement and more and more facsimiles and all they achieved as individuals were the traps and snake-pits of implants on the whole track.

To stand at last near the heights of discovered beingness has withered the sadness of standing on other men's bitter and, until now, probably unrewarded search. It was necessary to ransack the facsimiles,which are themselves one's sole inheritance for travail in the MEST universe, to discover the common denominators of facsimiles and to discover that they were only facsimiles, how they were created and how experience was impressed upon the individual. One might well have the feeling of having narrowly escaped a terrible tragedy when he views the thinness on which he stood to view this brink of oblivion, for it was obviously never intended that anyone should recover from participation or even spectatorship in or of the game called MEST universe. Dante's inscription above the portals of Hell might very well be written best on the gates of entrance into this universe.

The common denominator of all difficulty an individual

has in the MEST universe may be summed up under the heading "facsimiles." Originally, in his own universe, he used the mechanism of energy creation to make objects. In the MEST universe this ability reduces to the use of energy solely for the recording of data about the MEST universe so that one can agree with that data. And in this process lies death, not only as a body periodically but as a thetan.

What has commonly been mistaken for knowledge has been the MEST universe track of seeking agreement with the MEST universe by discovering all possible data about what one should do in order to agree with the MEST universe. The more data one achieved, the more facsimiles he had; the more facsimiles he had, the more MEST he was. It was necessary to win through this trap in order to recognize, isolate and evaluate the common denominators of facsimiles, and to discover that self-created energy has been utilized to enforce agreement upon oneself so as to enslave one's beingness and lead it to its final destruction.

No adventure in the MEST universe can exceed the adventure of making orderly anatomy from the chaos of commingled matter, energy and space which comprise the planets, galaxies and island universes of this Black Beyond which awaited to devour the universe self-constructed of any thetan or group of thetans. The slaying of a roaring beast of fire held in it, in olden times, less action and danger.

These lines are not written from any self-congratulatory motive, for fame is a rock. But by these lines the auditor may be impressed by the actuality of what he handles, and so that he can appreciate his own gallantry in fronting an adversary of such insentient brutality.

The road to knowledge led through the anatomy of the space and energy masses called the MEST universe. The data did not lie *in* the MEST universe. The ransacking of facsimiles for data about one's identity, about one's "past history" in the MEST universe, should be tolerated by the auditor only insofar as it gives him materials for creative processing. He should never directly begin the direct processing of facsimiles, whether engrams or secondaries, save only in the case of an assist. He needs only to know so much of a preclear's beingness on the whole track to know what to mock up for the preclear's running.

The difficulty the preclear is having is not so much the content of various facsimiles but, on this high echelon of Scientology on which we are now operating, the fact that he *has* facsimiles. The path of better techniques is the path toward permitting the preclear to step away from all his facsimiles.

The track to knowledge, then, has two directions. It is possible at this time to take the better path. The essence of true knowledge is the essence of existing so that one can create beingnesses and data to know. All other data are junior to this.

A control operation of some magnitude was once perpetrated in the late 18th century. It was stated with great authority that anything worth knowing would always be beyond the bounds of human experience. This sought, knowingly or unknowingly, further to block the search for beingness. It should never be considered by anyone or under any circumstances that anything which can affect him could be beyond his ability to know the full nature of what he is experiencing. If any lesson is contained in Scientology, it is the lesson that the gates to all knowingness are open.

One should have the knowledge of the composition of the MEST universe as a fox might have use for the knowledge of a trap. It is cruelty to make a theta clear without at the same time educating him so as to permit him to avoid those pitfalls which brought him where he is found—in a MEST body on a planet named Earth (Solar System, Galaxy 13, MEST Universe).

Top-scale knowing would be top-scale ability to create beingness. The identity assigned to one by others and the data contained in facsimiles are knowingness not worth having.

Cause-Full Effect

Above the level of all else on the Chart of Attitudes is Cause. Causation is the highest attainment which can be envisaged by the thetan, but this is not necessarily the highest possible attainment, and much higher levels may be envisionable by the thetan when he has attained high on the level of causation.

To be Full Cause, one would have to be able to cause space and many other manifestations. Everyone, to a greater or lesser degree, attempts to be cause until he is at last the full effect. The fullest effect in this universe is to be MEST itself.

One of the principles of causation is outlined in the cycle of action, but it is not necessarily true that one can only cause a cycle of this pattern or that one must cause cycles at all, for it is excellent processing to mock-up with reverse cycles going from death back to creation with objects which one has mocked up.

It is one of the "facts" of objects that space and energy must have been caused before the object could exist in the MEST universe. Thus any object has prior cause. For this reason when anyone in the MEST universe begins to study in order to resolve some of the riddles of the MEST universe, he falls into the trap of supposing all cause to be prior and time itself to exist. This would make one the later effect of everything he caused. In other words, if he made a postulate, he would then immediately afterwards become the effect of that postulate. Causes motivated by "future" desire, enforcement and inhibition of havingness, do not lie in the past but only in the condition of havingness in this universe which states that any object must have had a "prior" cause.

The preclear has become aberrated by the process of making an effect out of him and taking from him the ability to be cause by convincing him that it is better to be an effect.

Freud had one of the major aberrations in view when he declared his libido theory in 1894 and decided therein that sex was the only aberration. It is certainly a major one in homo sapiens, for in sex one desires to be the cause of little or nothing and desires to be the effect of pleasurable sensation.

Anything in the MEST universe which one desires, he desires because it will have a pleasant effect on him. Thus he is searching for sensation caused exterior to himself which will make on him an effect. How much of an effect can he become? MEST! The snare of pleasurable sensation leads one to accept energy other than one's own. Desire for this energy or objects then puts one in the condition of being an effect. When one is surrounded by as many powerful possible energy sources as one finds in the MEST universe, he cannot but become a low level cause.

When a preclear is at a level on the tone-scale where he is concerned with bad and good (above 8·0 both these are seen broadly enough to understand that they are viewpoints) he is very concerned if he thinks that he is or could be bad cause and is desirous of being what he considers good cause. He judges these things by moral codes and so bends his conduct as to make bad cause antipathetic to himself and others. Thus he gives away responsibility for bad cause and in that very action becomes the effect of bad cause. When he has found himself to be what he considers bad cause, he ceases to "trust" himself and begins to blame himself and then others.

All angels have two faces. They are commonly represented in mythology as having a black and white face. To be complete cause, theoretically, a person would have to be willing to be bad cause and good cause. Only in this wise, in the MEST universe, could he escape the liability of becoming the effect of bad cause.

The criminal who has elected himself bad cause through having found it impossible to trust himself (and a criminal career always begins at the moment when the criminal-to-be loses his self-respect; a career of prostitution cannot begin until self-respect is lost; and self-respect is only lost when one considers himself to be bad cause) can only escape becoming

69

an effect by fighting all good cause. The reformation or reclamation of the criminal does not depend upon punishment, which only seeks to make him more MEST than he is, nor yet upon good cause, which he must fight, but upon the reestablishment of the criminal's self-respect; for only after this is he capable of being good cause.

An entire process evolves around "what would you cause on (each one of the dynamics)?" An assessment of the preclear with a meter should seek to establish where the preclear feels he would be bad cause, for it is on this point that he will be found to have lost his self-respect and where it will be discovered why he cannot trust himself. Self-trust, self-respect and the ability to be cause are conditions in the same order of magnitude and can be interchangeably approached.

I Am—I Am Not

On the Chart of Attitudes which accompanies the *Handbook for Preclears*, it will be found at 22·0 "I am myself." The only true identity is "myself." It is not a name, it is not a designation. Orders, titles, ranks, praise and enduring fame alike do not bring about the condition "I am" or an actual identity; they bring about instead an identification, with all the liabilities of identification. The finality of identification is 0·0 or lower on the tone-scale.

The concept of infinite mind is not new, but it has always been assigned to another beingness than self. The preclear will be found to be intensely aberrated who has sworn allegiance to some infinite beingness and has then agreed that all space belonged to that beingness, and that the rights of creation and energy belonged to that beingness and did not belong to self. This is a handy and, to the very badly aberrated, acceptable method of denying any responsibility for anything. It is also the shortest route toward I AM NOT. Infinite mind is individualistic. All mankind does not depend upon or share a portion of the infinite mind. On the contrary, the highest individualism attainable is the individualism of the

70

infinite mind. It was beyond the power and grasp of the intellect applying itself to the field of philosophy, to conceive a multiplicity of infinite minds, and these commentators had agreed sufficiently with the MEST universe to conceive that the only space was the MEST universe space and they could not understand that this was an illusion, and that the existence of space does not depend upon existing space. Just as there can be an "infinity" of ideas, so can there be an "infinity" of "infinities" of space. Two beings theoretically, each with an infinite mind, and each capable of the production of an infinity of space, could yet co-produce sufficient space to communicate with each other. This may be difficult to conceive until one has attained a level of the tone-scale sufficient for an expansive viewing of his potentialities, at which moment it becomes simplicity itself.

There is a psychosis which has as its manifestation the illusion that one is God and the ruler of the universe. This psychosis comes about from the effort of an individual who is well below complete agreement with the MEST universe, to shift into the valence of what he has already accepted to be the creator of the universe. Instead of being himself, he has become unable even to be a MEST body in a sane condition, has conceived God to be MEST, and has then shifted into the valence of God. God, in this case, will be found to be conceived to be a MEST object. As an aside to this, below the level of complete agreement that the MEST universe is the only reality, begins the state which could be described by the statement, "I agree, I am still agreeing, and yet you are still punishing me." The unfortunate fact about the MEST universe is that it is MEST and is designed to punish and cares nothing about agreement with it beyond the point that one agrees with it, and has no spirit of fair play whereby punishment ceases when one has acknowledged the winner. Recognition of this brings on insanity in an effort to further back away from responsibility and further escape from punishment. In the MEST universe, this escape from punishment is, of course, impossible. Thus there is a level below 0·0 for any immortal being.

One of the first confusions on the part of the preclear which the auditor will encounter is the fact that the preclear considers himself to be in the state of I AM when he has a body and a name. This is high-tone compared to the sub-zero state in which the thetan quite often finds himself, but it is very far from optimum. Here the preclear is confusing identity with his own sense of beingness. His sense of beingness does not depend upon and, indeed, is confused by a MEST identity such as a name assigned to him and a body with which he can be recognized.

To a large degree the society of Earth requires, as part of its structure, names and the means to identify. The state finds itself very satisfied whenever it increases its ability to readily identify its citizenry, and will resort to almost any pretext to collect the fingerprints and dossier of one and all.

Identity is such a liability and is so thoroughly MEST that individuality is really not possible in the presence of sharply defined identity. Reaching down into the sub-zero tone-scale, the thetan finds it expedient not only to mask his be-ingness, but to hide his identity with great thoroughness even from himself. This passion for non-identity is the spasm of clinging to the last shreds of individuality which would other-wise be lost. Thetans from some of the corps operating in space have thoroughly agreed to be amongst themselves com-pletely black, the better to hide in the blackness of space. This blackness is found in the occluded case in many in-stances.

The commonest plea on the part of the preclear is "Who am I?" He feels that if he could only answer this, he would be happy. He then ransacks his facsimiles for all of his past identities on his many spirals and as these amount to hun-dreds of millions, he finds no surcease. He succeeds only in damaging himself with the many injuries contained in facsimiles through which he is searching. He is identifying to the point where he is searching not for the state of I AM but for WHAT HAVE I BEEN LABELLED? The attainment of the state of I AM depends upon one's ability to again be able to create space, energy and objects in and for his own universe, by himself or in co-operation with other thetans, and the rehabilitation of the many additional abilities of the thetan for the creation of energy is but one of a very large number. Thus the state of I AM is reached through creative processing and postulate processing rather than the processing of MEST universe facsimiles or endless searching with an E-meter to discover what one has been.

There are gods above all other gods. Anything which has wide acceptance and has been successful, wherever suns shine and planets swing, is based upon some fundamental truth. There is no argument here against the existence of a Supreme Being or any devaluation intended. It is that amongst gods, there are many false gods elected to power and position for the benefit and use of those who would control and make into the basest slaves the most sublime beings. As an ancient Greek said, when one has examined the descriptions of God written by men, he finds in that Being at best a thirst for self-aggrandizement and adulation which would be disgusting in any man. Man has sought to make his God a god of mud because the Early Greek and even more distant peoples, made idols in the form of men by which they thought to entrap the beingness of some local divinity who troubled them; more modern man has fallen into the error of making God into the body of a homo sapiens and posting him somewhere on high with a craving for vengeance and a pettiness in punishment matched only by the degradation of homo sapiens himself.

There are gods above all other gods, and gods beyond the gods of universes, but it were better, far better, to be a raving madman in his cell than to be a thing with the ego, cruelty, and jealous lust that base religions have set up to make men grovel down.

Win—Lose

It is noteworthy that as the preclear ascends the tone-scale, his desire to win increases. Those low on the tone-scale, even when they think they are trying to win, will almost uniformly set up their problems and solutions so that they will lose.

Homo sapiens has little converse with true competence. There is an astonishing level of winningness above 4·0 where competence becomes a joy like poetry.

Regret of competence ensues when one has employed competence to injure another being drastically. The duellist begins with joy in competence of sword-handling and before long, because of the counter-emotion he receives from his practice of the art, conceives disgust for competence. In a later life, he will carry this into everything he does, so fearing that he will employ competence to injure that he dares not practise competence in the smallest things; and by failing to practise competence, so introduces losingness, to the injury of himself and others. A man who instinctively recoils from competence and perfection, at the wheel of a car, will sometimes cause an accident rather than avoid one if competence of a high order is required in the avoidance.

To win one must wish to win; when one no longer desires to win, one no longer desires to live.

(*Note*—The remaining three columns of the chart of attitudes are covered broadly in the earlier text.)

The Emotional Scale and Sub-Zero Tone-Scale

The emotional scale has been covered often and exhaustively elsewhere. As has been discussed in this text, it is dependent upon that characteristic of energy known as affinity which itself is established by flows, dispersals and ridges.

Below zero on the tone-scale is applicable only to a thetan. It has been quite commonly observed that there are two positions for any individual on the tone-scale. This occurs because there is a position for the composite of the thetan plus his MEST body operating in a state of unknowingness that he is not a MEST body, and behaving according to social patterns, which give him some semblance of sanity. The other position on the tone-scale is the position of the thetan himself, and it is necessary for us to demonstrate a negative scale in order to find the thetan at all.

For the thetan you will find the scale as follows:

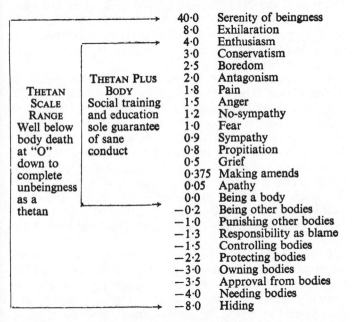

		40·0	Serenity of beingness
		8·0	Exhilaration
		4·0	Enthusiasm
		3·0	Conservatism
		2·5	Boredom
	THETAN PLUS	2·0	Antagonism
THETAN	BODY	1·8	Pain
SCALE	Social training	1·5	Anger
RANGE	and education	1·2	No-sympathy
Well below	sole guarantee	1·0	Fear
body death	of sane	0·9	Sympathy
at "O"	conduct	0·8	Propitiation
down to		0·5	Grief
complete		0·375	Making amends
unbeingness		0·05	Apathy
as a		0·0	Being a body
thetan		−0·2	Being other bodies
		−1·0	Punishing other bodies
		−1·3	Responsibility as blame
		−1·5	Controlling bodies
		−2·2	Protecting bodies
		−3·0	Owning bodies
		−3·5	Approval from bodies
		−4·0	Needing bodies
		−8·0	Hiding

This sub-zero tone-scale shows that the thetan is several bands below knowingness as a body, and so he will be found in the majority of cases. In our homo sapiens he will be discovered to be below zero on the tone-scale. The zero-to-four plus tone-scale was formulated on, and referred to, bodies and the activity of thetans with bodies. In order,

75

then, to discover the state of mind of the thetan, one must examine the sub-zero scale. He has some trained patterns as a body which make it possible for him to know and to be. As himself, he has lost all beingness, all pride, all memories and all self-determined ability, but yet has an automatic response-mechanism in himself which continues furnishing his energy.

EACH ONE OF THE ABOVE POINTS ON THE SCALE IS RUN AS POSITIVE AND NEGATIVE. Example: The beautiful sadness of needing bodies. The beautiful sadness of NOT needing bodies. The beauty of being responsible for bodies, the beauty of NOT being responsible for bodies. Each one is run as itself and then as the reverse with the addition of NOT.

The sub-zero to 40·0 scale is the range of the thetan. A thetan is lower than body death, since it survives body death. It is in a state of knowingness *below* 0·375 only when it is identifying itself as a body and IS, to its own thinking, the body. The BODY-PLUS-THETAN scale is from 0·0 to 4·0, and the position on this scale is established by the social environment and education of the composite being and is a stimulus-response scale. The preclear is initially above this 0·375 on the BODY-PLUS-THETAN range. Then, on auditing, he commonly drops from the FALSE TONE of the BODY-PLUS-THETAN scale and into the true tone of the thetan.

This is actually the only self-determined tone present— the actual tone of the thetan. From this sub-zero he quickly rises up scale through the entire range as a thetan and generally settles at 20·0 and in command of the body and situations. The course of auditing then takes the preclear, quite automatically, down from the FALSE TONE of the BODY-PLUS-THETAN scale to the actual tone of the thetan. Then the tone of the thetan rises back up the scale level by level.

It is not uncommon to find the preclear (who IS the thetan) quite raving mad under the false "veneer" of social and educational stimulus-response training and to discover that the preclear, while behaving quite normally in the BODY-PLUS-THETAN state, becomes irrational in the course of auditing. BUT DESPITE THIS, the preclear is actually being far more sane and rational than ever before and the moment he discovers himself as himself, as THE source of energy and personality and beingness of a body, he becomes physically and mentally better. Thus the auditor must not be dismayed at the course of tone, but should simply persevere until he has the thetan up into rational range. A raving mad thetan is far more sane than a normal human being. But then, as you audit, observe it for yourself.

The Dichotomies

While the auditor can do much solely by reducing facsimiles, he soon will find that his preclears are not always able to erase facsimiles easily. He will find occasionally that he often has a difficult time when a particularly heavy facsimile is in restimulation and, do what he will, the auditor may find his preclear's tone remains unchanged and that the preclear's attitudes have not evolved to a better high.

We now come to "The Governor" mentioned in a lecture in the autumn of 1951. The speed of a preclear is the speed of his production of energy.

The most important step in establishing a preclear's self-determinism, the main goal of the auditor, is the rehabilitation of the preclear's ability to produce energy.

A being is, apparently, an energy production source. How does he produce live energy without mechanical means, cellular activity, or food?

The basic principle of energy production by a being has been copied in electronics. It is very simple. A difference of potential of two areas can establish an energy flow of themselves. Carbon batteries, electric generators, and other producers of electrical flows act on the principle that a difference of energy potential in two or more areas can cause an electrical impulse to flow between or amongst them.

The preclear is static and kinetic, meaning he is no-motion and motion. These, interplaying, produce electrical flow.

A preclear as a static can hold two or more energy flows of different wavelengths in proximity and between them obtain a flow.

A preclear can hold a difference of flow between two waves and a static so long (and arduously) that the effect of a discharging condenser can be obtained. This can "explode" a facsimile.

The preclear flows electrical currents of command at the body. These hit pre-established ridges (areas of dense waves) and cause the body to perceive or act. The preclear takes perception from the body with tractor beams. He holds the body still or braces himself against it by wrapping a tractor (pulling) beam around it while he places a pressor (pushing) beam at his back to command himself into action. (You can almost break a preclear's spine by asking him to contract his own tractor around his body and yet withhold the pressor against his spine.)

All an auditor really needs to know about this is the elementary method of using a difference of potential. That creates energy.

The only thing wrong with a preclear with an aged MEST body is that he has too many facsimiles of his tractors and pressors handling his own MEST body and the rickety state of the body feeds back "slowness" so that he thinks his energy is low—and until worked with some method such as this, facsimiles do not reduce.

Any difference of potential played one against the other creates energy. Aesthetic waves against a static produce energy. Aesthetic waves against analytical waves produce energy. Analytical waves against emotional waves produce energy. Emotional waves against effort waves produce energy. Effort against matter produces energy.

The last is the method used on Earth in generating electrical current for power. The others are equally valid and produce even higher flows. This is a gradient scale of beingness, from the zero-infinity of theta to the solidity of matter.

The differences of potential most useful are easy to run.

This is, actually, alternating current running. There can be DC running or chain fission running but these are very experimental at this writing.

AC is created by the static holding first one, then the other, of a dichotomy of two differences of potential. A flow is run in one direction with one of the pair, then in the other direction with the other.

The dichotomies are:

1. Survive
   Succumb
2. Affinity
   No affinity
3. Communication
   No communication
4. Agree
   Disagree
5. Start
   Stop
6. Be
   Be not
7. Know
   Know not
8. Cause
   Effect
9. Change
   No change
10. Win
    Lose
11. I am
    I am not
12. Faith
    Distrust
13. Imagine
    Truth
14. Believe
    Not believe
15. Always
    Never
16. Future
    Past
17. Everyone
    Nobody
18. Owns all
    Owns nothing
19. Responsible
    Not responsible
20. Right
    Wrong
21. Stay
    Escape
22. Beauty
    Ugliness

23. Reason
    Emotion

24. Emotion
    Effort

25. Effort
    Apathy

26. Acceptance
    Rejection

How are these used?

27. Sane
    Insane

28. No sympathy
    Sympathy

29. Sympathy
    Propitiation

And the state of Static, a motionlessness sometimes necessary to run.

One asks the preclear to flow agreement, then disagreement. He flows a feeling, a thought (NEVER the phrase!) of "agreement" out or in, in the direction he chooses relative to himself. He lets this flow until it turns smoky grey or white, then black. Then he changes the direction of flow and gets the thought or feeling of "disagreement". He runs this until it turns grey or white, then black. When this has turned black or dark, he again runs "agreement" in its direction until he gets grey or white, then again black. Now he reverses the flow and flows the thought "disagreement" until he gets grey or white, then blackness. And so on and on.

It will be noted that at first it may take some little time for a flow to run from black through white to black. As the preclear continues to run, after minutes or many hours, he begins to run faster, then faster and faster, until at last he can keep a flow blazing and crackling.

A method of aberrating beings was to give them white and black energy sources in their vicinity. These show up on a very low tone occluded case as blazing white and shining white. That is an electronic incident, not his own energy flow. These run blazing white *in one direction* for minutes or hours before they go black. They then run the other way, blazing white, almost as long.

WHEN BLACK PREDOMINATES IN SUCH INCIDENTS THEY DO NOT DIMINISH OR REDUCE. ASK THE PRECLEAR IN SUCH A CASE TO DO

WHAT HE "HAS TO DO" TO GET THE INCIDENT ALL WHITE.

As the preclear runs, he finds the speed of the change of flow changes, more and more rapidly until it runs like a vibration. This vibration, theoretically, can increase to a strong current which becomes so great it is well to *ground* your preclear by using an E-meter or letting him hold a wire in each hand which is connected to a bare water pipe or radiator. Otherwise, his MEST body may be damaged by the flow.

Run a dichotomy only against its mate. Run in alternating directions until the flow turns black.

Don't run a black "flow." It doesn't flow or run out.

Methods of Running

There are many methods of running facsimiles and of handling ridges and flows. These have been covered in other publications; all of them have validity and can advance cases.

In the present publication there are only two processes which are stressed and these processes are superior to others published prior to December 1st, 1952. A great many tests have established the fact that two processes, both of them simple, produce far better results than any of the others.

The title "Scientology 8-8008" means the attainment of infinity by the reduction of the MEST universe's apparent infinity to zero and the increase of the zero of one's own universe to an infinity of one's own universe. This road is attained by postulate processing and creative processing.

To run any incident or use any process it is necessary for the auditor to have a very sound idea of what he is doing, and to this end it is recommended that he know and be able to use the following:

Processing

The Code
The Theta Entity

Postulate Processing

Actually energy is produced by the thetan simply by postulating that it will be in existence. What he says will be so, becomes so for him; if he becomes extremely powerful, it becomes so for others. This condition has been misused by most thetans who, often in the past, have been afraid of making postulates that will come true. They believe that if they say a thing will happen, it will then happen—to such an extent that they now revulse against stating anything will happen.

Another aberrative condition with regard to postulates is that for the sake of randomity, the thetan at some time or another has set up the postulate that every time he makes a postulate a reverse postulate will occur which he will not know about, in such a way that he can "play chess with himself" without spoiling the game by knowing what his left hand is doing when his right makes the move.

It is not true that postulates have to be located all through the facsimiles and worn out by repetition. It is just as easy to make new postulates; but first one must recover from the depths to which his postulates have taken him. The most dangerous postulates are those postulates where one decided to agree with something which would become aberrative.

You can see by examining any facsimile in the preclear related to an accident that the most aberrative things in that facsimile are what the preclear himself decided.

Postulates are accompanied by evaluations and conclusions. It is often possible to "loosen" a postulate by discovering to the preclear why he made it, or what data he was using at the time.

As a preclear becomes very aberrated and believes himself to be more and more MEST, his postulates become as unwieldy to use as actual objects, and he finds them as difficult to change as objects.

When doing creative processing and moving objects and energy in created space and time, the preclear is doing this by making postulates. It comes as a shock to some preclears that they are handling time by shifting space. One handles time by simply saying that he had a thing and now he does not have it, or that he will have or will view a thing in the future. One does not shift time by shifting space, nor does one continue to look at something he has put into the past. He says it is in the past and so it becomes in the past.

When the thetan is unable to handle postulates about time, the auditor should ask him about some MEST universe incident such as breakfast, and then enquire how he remembered that he had breakfast, and if he will have something to eat on the morrow, and then how he knows he will have something to eat on the morrow. He does not look at his breakfast to find out if he had breakfast, he *knows* that he ate breakfast; and he does not go into tomorrow to find out if he will probably eat on the morrow, he *knows*—or, at least, believes it possible—that he will eat on the morrow. Moving time, as in any other postulate, is knowingness not viewingness. An object goes into the past in the same space as it was in, in the present; and in the future may be in the same space as it was in in the past. The space does not change:

the condition of havingness changes, and one estimates this by some degree of knowingness.

The entire subject of postulates is the subject of certainty and self-belief. That preclear who has a low self-belief finds it difficult first, to make a postulate which he will believe and second, to undo one he has made. Creative processing and postulate processing alike remedy this.

Rising-scale processing is another way of doing postulate processing. One takes any point or column of the Chart of Attitudes as given in this text, which the preclear can reach, and asks the preclear then to shift his postulate upwards toward a higher level.

In order to do this the auditor says, *"Now, on the subject of rightness and wrongness, how wrong do you think you generally are?"* The preclear tells him. The auditor says, *"How high can you shift this attitude toward believing yourself right?"* The preclear shifts the attitude as high as he can. The auditor takes this as the next level from which he will work upward until he attains as nearly as possible a postulate which will "hold" to the effect that the preclear believes himself right. Rising-scale processing should not be confused with the processing of flows. One can process all these columns in terms of flows. Rising-scale processing is simply a method of shifting postulates upward toward optimum from where the preclear believes he is on the chart. Rising-scale processing is essentially a process directed toward increasing belief in self by using all the "buttons" on the Chart of Attitudes.

The preclear is generally found to be quite uncertain about his postulates. He does not know whether or not what he says will take effect or, if he says it and if it takes effect, if it will not rebound upon him. He becomes afraid to make postulates for fear he will make some postulate destructive to himself or others and may even discover himself making postulates to convince himself he should be ill.

One has to tell oneself what to be before one' is. Recovery of this ability is the essence of processing a thetan.

Postulate processing is a very vital process to apply to the thetan: when he is exteriorized, he can change his postulates rapidly. If he finds himself thinking slowly and doing other things which are not optimum when he is outside, one can better his situation and condition by asking him to change postulates.

Creative Processing

Standard Operating Procedure for theta clearing is the backbone of processing in Scientology. It is easily followed but the auditor should have an excellent command of all types of processing in order to use it more successfully.

SOP is most easily done and most successfully by an auditor who is a theta clear. Auditors who are not theta clear seldom understand it, and a low-toned uncleared auditor who cannot himself leave his body very often acts to pin a preclear inside his body. It is noteworthy that many auditors have been unable to obtain successes with theta clearing before they themselves have been cleared, but immediately after the auditor was cleared, he was successful with each successive case without exception. The fear of some thetans from various causes of leaving the body causes the auditor—who is the thetan—to make other thetans stay in bodies, and it is actually quite dangerous to be audited by auditors who are not theta clears. The process is not dangerous; uncleared auditors are.

Standard Operating Procedure, Issue 3

This process is done in steps. The auditor with EVERY preclear makes no other judgment than to begin with Step I and, failing to accomplish that immediately, to go to Step II;

if he fails to accomplish this immediately, he goes to Step III; and so on. When he is able to accomplish a step he labels the case as that step number, i.e., a III. He then begins working with that step. After a few hours' work, he again starts at the top with the preclear with Step I and progresses on through. Eventually the preclear becomes a Step I.

STEP I—POSITIVE EXTERIORIZING: Ask the preclear to be a foot back of his head. If he does, make him go back further, then up, then down, practising placement in space and time. Then one asks him to see if there are any items in the body he would like to repair and proceeds to let the preclear repair them according to the preclear's own ideas as to how he should do it. Then educate the preclear by making him create and destroy his own illusions into finally getting a certainty of illusion and from this a certainty of perceiving the real universe with all perceptions. (Note: The most real universe is, of course, one's own illusory universe and should be completely rehabilitated before one attempts to perceive or handle or worry about the MEST universe. Rehabilitated, sonic, visio, etc. of the MEST universe are very clear and very certain. Clear perception in early stages is not a test of being outside. The only test is whether the preclear KNOWS he is outside.) Failing the first line of this step, go to Step II.

STEP II—BY ORIENTATION: Ask the preclear, still inside, to locate the inside of his forehead. Ask him to put a pressor beam against it and push himself out the back of his head. Supplement this by asking him to reach out through the back of his head and grab the wall with a pulling beam and pull himself out. Ask him to steady himself outside and then, by means of beams, to raise and lower himself while outside and to move to various parts of the room while still outside. Use creative processing. By orientation as a thetan, placing himself as a thetan in time and space, he becomes sure of his whereabouts. Have him find and cast off old lines which have their terminals fixed to him. Have him find those lines

86

wherever they are and attach them to radiators and water taps as the energy will drain out of him. (The II ordinarily has enough lines to cause him to snap back in the head when he releases beams.) Failing this, go to Step III.

STEP III—SPACE PROCESSING: In that the MEST universe has forced upon the thetan its spatial dimensions and directions, the thetan is likely to become a point which is being subjected to all the counter-efforts and counter-emotions of his environment, for his entire concept of space is being determined by the MEST universe. Have the thetan, still inside, find his feet in the opposite direction from where the MEST body is located by the MEST universe. Have him turn the feet around. Have him create differences in his body and reverse various limbs and positions according to his viewpoint, each one in disagreement with the MEST universe, particularly as appertaining to gravity and other influences. This sets up an ability to disagree with the MEST universe in terms of space. Have him locate his eyes in the back of his head, on the soles of his feet and in other places. Have him assume other bodies, each time changing them slightly, and putting them away. Then have him gather himself into his normal MEST universe spatial areas and go to Step I.

STEP IV—RIDGE RUNNING: Ask the preclear to give himself a command to walk. Let him locate the white flow line which results inside his head. When this line goes dark, have him locate the tiny ridge inside the skull that stopped it. Have him run the flow from this barrier (these barriers, are tiny ridges and each has a thought with it such as *"Can't walk"* or *"Too bored to walk"*) back toward the spot where he told himself to walk. It will run white for a moment, then go black. Have him give himself the command to walk again and "watch" this flow line. It may run through two or three tiny barriers and then stop. Again have him run the "objection" to walking. Have him watch this "objection" flow until it goes black. Then have him give himself the command to walk again and so on and so on. He will wind up at some outside point. Now have him give himself the command *"Listen"* and have him run this and its back flows on "black and white" until he is exterior on the subject of listen. Then use the command *"Talk"* similarly. Then the command *"Nod,"* then the command *"Move,"* etc. Give *"Look"* last for it may "blind" his perception of black and white. He may each time get out to a distance in another quarter. If he can do all this, start with Step I again. Failing this step, failing to "see" black and white energy manifestations, go to Step V.

STEP V—BLACK AND WHITE CONTROL PROCESSING: Give the preclear a complete E-meter assessment, using the principles of what he would create or destroy or would not create and would not destroy. Use this data to make mock-ups. Then have the preclear create and perceive black spots and then white spots, black crosses and white crosses, and move these here and there through the room or through his own space. Turn them on and off, interchange them, put them in yesterday, put them in tomorrow, make them get larger, make them get smaller; each time doing as much as the preclear can do. Each time one asks him to perceive one of his own created illusions in terms of black and white spots or crosses, one attempts to coax him into successful control of it. Audit very persuasively and lightly. This preclear ordinarily is frightened of blackness because it either can contain dangerous things or contains nothing, and he cannot differentiate which. Thus he cannot control blackness and, in being unable to control blackness, flounders in it. He also has a more basic computation: that blackness is the only safe thing in which to hide and, therefore, blackness is a thing to have. Further, blackness "takes" things for him. This preclear may be afraid of the police, may believe himself to have a hideous body, thetawise, and has many other reasons why he cannot exteriorize. Drills on creating and perceiving black and white should be continued until he can handle each easily. The trouble with this preclear and preclears lower than this is that they have agreed too heavily with the MEST universe and must be very cautious in confronting it, since in that direction they conceive to lie a much more complete defeat even than that from which they are now suffering. Audit him also very heavily on Creative Processing.

Then go through steps again. If the preclear is immediately perceived to have little or no reality on ANY incident, go to Step VI.

STEP VI—ARC STRAIGHT WIRE: Drill, by direct questioning, on locks until the preclear can remember something really "real" to him, something which he "really loved," something with which he was in communication. Then drill him on creating illusions until he is certain he has created one which really isn't real, which he is certain HE put the emotion and perceptions into. Then go through steps again. Failing Step VI after a quick test, go to Step VII.

STEP VII—PRESENT TIME BODY ORIENTATION: Have preclear locate a part of his body and recognize it as such. Have him locate furniture, fixtures, auditor in room. Have him locate the town and country he is in. Get him to find something in present time which is really real to him, with which he can communicate. Work on this until he can do this. Then go to Step VI. Then go to Step I.

General Processing

Anything which rehabilitates the self-determinism of a preclear, whether education, change of environment, running facsimiles, theta clearing or the creation of one's own universe, is valid processing. Any one of these will raise the tone of the preclear markedly.

At the end of 80,000 hours of investigation of beingness in the MEST universe, I have concluded that those processes which make it possible for the preclear to disagree with the MEST universe also make it possible for him to handle the MEST universe, or to create his own or be part of a group which creates a universe, as the case may be. Scientology

8–8008 is remarkable for its ability to better the beingness and action potentials of the individual. It is, sadly enough, the only technique which I have seen produce excellent and fast results in the hands of trained auditors. Mainly the reason is that homo sapiens has and will continue to use, any technique delivered into his hands for the control and enslavement of others, for homo sapiens is frightened. Even when an auditor was competent with earlier techniques, it would often occur that his preclear would return into his past environment and would relapse. This occurred because others had a vested interest in the preclear's continuation in a state of aberration; and others would lose no moment in starting again to crush this preclear down the tone-scale to a point where they conceived he was more easily controlled. Mest is the most easily controlled item in the MEST universe, and the closer a human being could be pressed toward MEST, the easier, it was thought, to control him. That his value and ethical sense deteriorated in direct ratio to the degree he was depressed down the tone-scale, was overlooked by the homo sapiens who had a passion for slavery. The primary benefit of Scientology 8–8008 is that it works so swiftly even when indifferently used that the persons in the environment of the preclear are over-reached rapidly by the preclear and find themselves subject to his control when they act to continue his aberration. Further the auditor is seldom aware of the height his preclear attains until the preclear has attained it. Processing has always worked in the hands of a competent auditor; and it were better for any technique, no matter how dangerous, to be known to Man if it could benefit at least a few, for homo sapiens has no psycho-therapy. In Dianetics he had his first thoroughly validated psychotherapy and Dianetics worked and still works uniformly in the hands of those skilled in its application. In Scientology in general, and in theta clearing in particular, the upper limits of homo sapiens as such have been transcended and it would not be good semantics to call a theta clear a homo sapiens or even, exactly speaking, a person, for he is a thetan with a body he uses for purposes of action and communication, and his viewpoint is quite altered. His general health is more or less directly under his control, but there is no goal for the body as a final goal in Scientology, for the body is a tool. The genetic entity which built the human body *really* wanted to be served. The complexities and ridges which he developed speak of a craving for energy and self-service which could only be the basest aberration, and, true enough, the genetic entity is aberrated almost beyond belief, as any thetan discovers when he seeks to clear the genetic entity. The body is quite alive and self-motivated without the thetan, as the thetan soon discovers; but it is so used to taking orders from successive lines of thetans which themselves some day would probably become part of this complex system of ridges, that its "mental activities" are quite stupid. The thetan who has lived in this association and has believed himself to be the body is early quite appalled at the character of the genetic entity who is cowardly, a thing of stimulus-response, without further will or goals than to grow a body, and obsessed entirely with the idea of growing one. The thetan can repair the body quite easily if he so chooses, but quite often sees it as a pointless activity; for one's personality is not even faintly dependent upon the body but is only debased by association with one. When one has learned to control a body from a distance, he is usually content to let it get along as best it can, for the reduction of all counter-efforts of the genetic entity would be a reduction of the entire body. The genetic entity has his whole track and has had his own travails. In other parts of space, not too incredibly, "dolls" are used by thetans—things which can be animated easily by theta energy and which are disposable and which do not have the uncomfortable circumstance of being themselves any more alive than any other MEST.

The MEST universe itself has a considerable cravingness in it. It is composed of energy which was emanated in order to have, and the energy still contains as its basic characteristic Have and Not Have, and is itself, when contacted, found to possess a craving which does not make the MEST alive but which speaks of that which made the MEST. This craving-ness is an essential part of all matter. Certain metals contain the desire to be had much more than others, and certain other metals contain the craving not to be had. This is one way of looking at positive and negative reactions. The body's being composed of such energy makes it feel as though it is holding on to the thetan. Nothing is really holding on to the thetan since he has no substance which can be held. Even the genetic entity does not hold on to the thetan, but probably considers him some sort of far off commanding god—if he thinks of the thetan at all.

Space has its own demanding quality and insists on its dimensions being accepted by anything in the universe, for it was erected and is erected on a command basis in the MEST universe.

Processing must resolve this havingness on the part of matter, and the commandingness on the part of space. To confront these directly is, for most preclears, an impossibility, for it only drives them further into an apathy of agreement with MEST. The preclear has long contested with the MEST universe and has continually sought to create his own universe only to find the MEST universe declaring itself stronger each time and compressing the illusion to nothing.

The war cry of the MEST universe is: "Must have gotten it somewhere," and "It must have gone somewhere." It will not tolerate the vaguest possibility that one created himself or could destroy anything himself. The whole sub-zero scale is a manifestation of one's efforts to combat this demanding-ness on the part of the MEST universe. Hiding, protecting, owning, are all mechanisms to answer the question, "Where did you get it?" "What did you do with it?" The MEST universe, in this light, is essentially a police universe, for it operates upon force and intolerance and demands with pain that its laws be accepted. In that its laws are based solely upon agreement, it is only necessary to discover how one can disagree with them to abolish what has been called "natural law" for oneself. Upon the abolishment of this agreement depends the health, progress and advancement of the thetan. This universe is a major expanding trap of finite dimensions and rather idiotic simplicity. If one were to leave the MEST universe, one would solely create space of his own and maintain enough knowledge of what could happen with regard to the MEST universe to defeat its encroachment and its salesmen. No universe, however cunningly constructed, is entirely proof against this expanding trap. The MEST universe is a game which has gone on too long and of which even the players are tired. Earth could be considered to be at this time an egress terminal.

It is noteworthy that one must not accept or know any of these conditions to have these processes work. They act very swiftly and uniformly on any homo sapiens and upon other beings. A considerable number of the principles which have been discovered in Scientology exist above the MEST universe. The MEST universe itself might be considered to be the "inevitable average" of illusion once it starts in a certain direction. We have in natural law as applied to the MEST universe the sum of agreement upon illusion. Tracing the principles of Scientology as they apply specifically to the MEST universe, is the tracing of the agreements which brought about the MEST universe. The axioms of 1951 are, in the main, a tracing of this agreement. The inevitability and "diabolical accuracy" of these predictions of human behaviour depend upon their being held in common by Man, which they are. They extend as well to other beings below the level of player in this universe and have applied to many sets of players, while much of the data which has been recovered in this investigation seems, to the narrow scope of homo sapiens, quite wild, the wildness depends on the absence of investigation in the past and can be compared only to the stupidity which remained ignorant of them; for these matters were an unseen and insidious causation underlying the grief of Earth, at best a pawn in a minor game in a minor galaxy.

The Anatomy of Space

Before energy can exist in this universe, space must exist. His inability to create space is one of the most aberrative characteristics of the thetan whom we find in a MEST body. He has become reduced to a point even in his own concept, and perhaps even less than a point for he has no space of his own but must depend upon bodies and other conditions to believe that he has space.

It is of the utmost importance for the auditor to understand space. Space can be considered to be a viewpoint of dimensions. It does not matter how many dimensions there are or what conditions are set up for these dimensions: the resulting condition is known as "space." There are only three dimensions in space in the MEST universe. Throughout all of its galaxies it has only length, breadth and depth. Space warps and other things of equal interest can exist in one's own universe, but they do not exist as such, evidently, in the MEST universe.

The assignation of dimension is the essence of space, but even before dimension can be assigned, one must have viewpoint. If one is assigning dimension from his viewpoint, he is cause; if dimension is being assigned to his viewpoint, he is effect. He is cause or effect to the degree that he can assign dimension and call it space.

The preclear has a viewpoint and is the centre of that viewpoint. Splitting his attention often finds him occupying several viewpoints. He is capable of assuming many. Where he is aware of being aware is, however, his central viewpoint; and, although this may be communicated with or interlocked to some other viewpoint which he could call his own—even on some other planet or here on earth—he is yet as himself the centre of assignation of dimension where he is and as he is.

In many preclears this becomes so blurred that he does not know whether he is in or out of the body. Here even the

centre of viewpoint has been overridden by MEST assignation of dimension.

An essential in agreement with any illusion is the acceptance of the dimensions it assigns or that one may assign to it.
Space is no more complicated than this, but when a preclear
has been overridden by enforced assignation of dimension to
an enormous degree, his own viewpoint may be found to be
scattered or dispersed. It is this condition which finds the
preclear unable to tell whether he is in or out of his body;
when this condition exists he is in the state of being incapable
of confronting the MEST universe, even to the point of assert-
ing the ownership of a centre of viewpoint.

The solution of this problem is simple, in principle, although it may require many hours of auditing. Where the
preclear has a certainty of centre of viewpoint he exteriorizes
immediately and can become a theta clear in a very few hours;
when he has been compressed by counter-efforts and emotions
into an acceptance of MEST dimension to the point where
he cannot even be certain of a centre of viewpoint, it is necessary to recover this centre of viewpoint in order to recover a
point from which space can be assigned and, even more im-
portantly to the auditor, where the preclear can be exteriorized
easily and in a knowing condition.

One of the first "tricks" in auditing is to get the preclear
to look from the centre of his head at his environment and the
room. He very often sees it clearly and as it is and does, by
this, adjust his vision to see through his ridges. Even an
occluded case can sometimes do this, and can then be exteriorized rapidly. The next "trick" is to find some segment of the
environment which the preclear can see and ask him what is
in the areas where he can see nothing or does not wish to see.
He will say this or that may be in these areas. The auditor
then has him create those things or change those things and
shift those things which he is afraid may be in those areas
until he is no longer interested, at which time he can envision
the actual surroundings. By continuing this "trick" of rehabilitation of potential occupation of space (for a preclear

will not occupy space which he considers dangerous), the preclear may be found to exteriorize suddenly and sometimes with violence. In such a case he believes himself to be occupying yet another space, hiding perhaps in the darkness of deep MEST space, as well as in a body. Routine orientation and creative processing remedies this.

By making the preclear alter the body he is occupying, making mock-ups which he superimposes and changes around in disagreement with the MEST universe—upside down and right side up—he becomes better able to have a viewpoint from which he can create space or from which he can at least handle MEST universe space.

The preclear who does not exteriorize readily is not sure he is here at all and, indeed, he may be co-occupying other areas. A study of the preclear with the E-meter, locating him in other spaces and bringing him into the space where he is being audited, can best be done with creative processing, not by running facsimiles, for these only make him disperse even further. This preclear often has difficulties with time and has space confused with time. Time is not handled by moving space; time is handled simply by having and not having. The MEST universe insists that anything that disappears must have gone somewhere; thus the preclear is saddled with the belief that he must create space to put things in whenever time changes. Having the preclear conceive time change in the space which he occupies by refusing to let him go on looking at it in yesterday or to see it in tomorrow, but simply making him know that it is now in yesterday and the space is the same, does much to rehabilitate his orientation.

Drills in which space is assigned are highly beneficial to any preclear, and particularly so to those preclears who do not exteriorize readily or who cannot easily find themselves when they are out of their body. Simply have the preclear disagree with dimensions round him and see them with purposeful, creative distortion and he will at length focalize his viewpoint so that he can handle space and *know* that he is the centre. A being can be knowingly in many places but being

scattered into many places unknowingly is the worst of conditions.

Creation and Destruction

Self-determinism seeks as its goal the attainment of the
goal of theta itself.

Theta has the capability of locating matter and energy in
time and space and of creating time and space.

Any action requires space and time, for space and time are
necessary to motion.

Motion can be defined as change of location in space, and
any change of location requires time.

Thus we have an inter-acting triangle, one corner of which
could be labelled space, another corner time, and the third
energy. Matter is not included in the triangle because matter
is apparently cohesion and adhesion of energy.

The cycle of a universe could be said to be the cycle of
creation, growth, conservation, decay and destruction. This
is the cycle of an entire universe or any part of that universe;
it is also the cycle of life forms.

This would compare to the three actions of energy which
are Start, Change and Stop, where creation is Start, growth
is enforced Change, conservation and decay are inhibited
Change and destruction is Stop.

The two extremes of the cycle—creation and destruction
or, in the terms of motion, Start and Stop—are inter-dependent and are consecutive.

There could be no creation without destruction; as one
must eradicate the tenement before building the apartment
house, so, in the material universe, must destruction and
creation be intermingled. A good action could be said to be
one which accomplished the maximal construction with minimal destruction; a bad action could be said to be one which
accomplished the minimal construction with maximal
destruction.

That which is started and cannot be stopped and that
which is stopped without being permitted to run a course,

are alike actions bordering upon the psychotic. Unreasonableness itself is defined by persistence in one or the other of these courses of starting something which cannot be stopped (as in the case of an A-bomb) or of stopping something before it has reached a beneficial stage.

Unlimited creation without any destruction would be insane; unlimited destruction without any creation would be similarly insane.

In actuality, insanity can be grouped and classified, detected and remedied by a study of creation and destruction.

An individual will not be responsible for that on which he will not use force. The definition of responsibility is entirely within this boundary. That person will not be responsible in that sphere where he cannot tolerate force, and if one discovers in an individual where he will not use force, he will find where that individual will also refuse to be responsible.

An assessment of a case can be done by use of the accompanying graph. We see here creation with an arrow pointing straight downward and find there the word *insane,* and, under this, we list the dynamics. Wherever along any of these dynamics the individual cannot conceive himself to be able to create, on that level he will be found aberrated to the degree that he does not believe himself able to create. This might be thought to introduce an imponderable but such is not the case, for the individual is most aberrated on the first dynamic and, rightly or wrongly, conceives that he could not create himself. This goes to the extent, in homo sapiens, of believing that one cannot create a body and, rightly or wrongly, one is then most aberrated on the subject of his body.

Potentially, because of the character of theta itself, an individual in an absolute and possibly unattainable state, should be able to create a universe. Certainly it is true that every man is his own universe and possesses within himself all the capabilities of a universe.

To the extreme right of the graph we have the word

destroy and an arrow pointing downwards toward insanity and, beneath this, the list of the dynamics. That individual who can only destroy along any of these dynamics and cannot or will not create could be said to be aberrated on that dynamic. He is aberrated to the degree that he would destroy that dynamic.

CREATE	GROW CONSERVE DECAY	DESTROY
START	CHANGE	STOP
DIFFERENTIATE	ASSOCIATE	IDENTIFY
BE	DO	HAVE
SPACE	ENERGY	MATTER
40·0	20·0	0·0
If only this insane on subject	If only this still sane on subject	If only this insane on subject

Dynamic 1	Dynamic 1	Dynamic 1
Dynamic 2	Dynamic 2	Dynamic 2
Dynamic 3	Dynamic 3	Dynamic 3
Dynamic 4	Dynamic 4	Dynamic 4
Dynamic 5	Dynamic 5	Dynamic 5
Dynamic 6	Dynamic 6	Dynamic 6
Dynamic 7	Dynamic 7	Dynamic 7
Dynamic 8	Dynamic 8	Dynamic 8

Looking again at the column of creation, one finds the individual aberrated anywhere along the dynamics in that column where the individual will only create and will not destroy.

In the destruction column, one finds the individual aberrated on any dynamic in that column where he will not destroy.

In the middle ground of the graph, we find that a balance of creation and destruction is sanity, and in the dynamics below it we find the individual sane wherever he will create and destroy.

Use of this graph and these principles enable the auditor to assess hitherto hidden compulsions and obsessions on the part of the preclear. This is an auditing graph. If one looks at it another way than that of an auditor, he finds there laid out what has been occasionally posed as a philosophy of existence. Friedrich Nietzsche, in his book "Thus Spake Zarathustra," presents as a desirable code of conduct unlimited willingness to destroy. Philosophically the graph has little or no workability. In order to survive in any universe, conduct must be regulated by a sense of ethics. Ethics are possible on a reasonable level only when the individual is high on the tone-scale. In the absence of such height, ethics are supplanted by morals, which can be defined as an arbitrary code of conduct not necessarily related to reason. Should one attempt to regulate his conduct on the basis of unlimited creation or destruction, he would find it necessary to act entirely without judgment to put his philosophy into effect. It is noteworthy that the late Nazi regime can serve as a clinical test of the workability of a scheme of things wherein unlimited creation and destruction are held as an ideal. I heard a rumour lately that Adolf Hitler was dead.

Be, Have and Do

The physicist has long been on a carousel with regard to the component parts of the material universe.

He has had to define time in terms of space and energy, space in terms of time and energy, and energy in terms of time and space, and matter as a combination of all three. When three factors exist at such an altitude in a science, there can be no further clarification unless the material can be related to experience of an equal magnitude.

The current definition in Scientology has this liability: if self-determinism is the location of matter and energy in time and space, and the creation, change and destruction of time and space, then there is no comparable data by which to evaluate this level. The physicist has found the inter-relationship of time, space and energy to be invaluable and has, indeed, produced a civilization from this inter-relationship. Just as, with our definition of self-determinism, it is possible to de-aberate an individual and increase his potentialities in a way never before suspected possible, and with a speed which exceeds all past estimates even in the science of Scientology.

Because we are now working from a higher understanding than time, space and energy, it is possible to compare these to experience in such a way as to broaden their use and modify their force or increase it. Control of time, space and energy comes now well within our capabilities.

Space, time and energy in experience become Be, Have and Do, the component parts of experience itself.

Space could be said to be BE. One can *be* in a space without change and without time; one can also be, without action.

The essence of time is apparently possession. When possession ceases, the record of time ceases. Without possession change cannot be observed; in the presence of possession change can be observed. Thus it is deduced that time and possession are inter-dependent.

The past could be sub-divided into Had, Should Have Had, Did Not Have, and Got, Should Have Gotten, Did Not Get, and Gave, Should Have Given, Did Not Give.

The present could be sub-divided into Have, Should Have, Do Not Have, and Giving, Should Be Giving, Not Giving, and Receiving, Should Be Receiving, Not Receiving.

The future is sub-divisible into Will Have, Should Have, Will Not Have, and Getting, Will Be Getting, Will Not Be Getting, and Will Receive, Will Not Receive.

In each of the above, past, present and future, the word would apply for any individual or any part of the dynamics to all the other dynamics.

The way one knows there was a past is by knowing the conditions of the past. The most revelatory of these is the facsimile which was taken in the past. However, without any important possession in the present stemming forward from

the past, the past becomes unimportant; or, because possession ceased, the past is obliterated. The single matter of the
body of a past life not being in the present life invalidates the
existence of the past life to the individual who then does not
—or does not care to—remember it. Yet the facsimiles can
be nevertheless effective upon him.

Similarly the individual does not conceive to any extent
time, past the death of his body, since he will have no body.

Energy, whether in the field of thought, emotion or effort,
can be summed into DO. It requires beingness and havingness in order to achieve doingness. Here we have the static
of space acting against the kinetic of possession to produce
action in the field of thought, emotion or effort, the various
categories of doingness.

Should one care to test this as a process on a preclear, he
will find that the missing portions of the preclear's past have
to do with loss of something. Loss itself is the single most
aberrative factor in living. It has long been known in this
science that the release of a grief charge was an important
single improvement in the preclear. Grief is entirely and
only concerned with loss or threatened loss. Pain itself can
be defined in terms of loss, for pain is the threat which tells
one that loss of mobility or a portion of the body or the
environment is imminent. Man has pain so thoroughly
identified with loss that in some languages the words are
synonymous.

Loss is always identified with HAVE, for if one doesn't
have, one cannot lose.

The Hindu sought to depart into his Nirvana by refusing
to have anything to do with having. He sought thus to pro-
mote himself into Being. He saw that so long as he retained
a grasp on a body in any degree he was Having, and thus was
pressed into Doing.

Having and Being are often identified to the degree that
many people attempt exclusively to Be only by Having. The
capitalist judges his own beingness solely by the degree of

possession, not even vaguely by the degree of action he is able to execute.

Possessions absorb and enforce time; only without possessions would one be able to regulate time at will. This is a singular attribute of the cleared theta clear, and to him possession of MEST is extremely unimportant.

One can make up for a lack of Having by Doing, and by Doing accomplishes Having and thus regulates time.

Having enhances either Being or Doing, as is sometimes severely recognized by one who would like to take a vacation or a trip to foreign lands.

Doing can enhance either Being or Having: a balanced Doing slants in both directions, but if one does without Having, his Being increases, as is well-known by anyone who insists on doing favours without recompense, and without gain.

There is an optimum speed of Doing. If one travels less than that speed he has little Being and Having; if one travels greater than that speed, he has to abandon both Being and Having. This is applicable especially to the MEST universe. The case of a race driver is in point. He must assume a contempt for Being and Having in order to achieve the speeds he does.

When change is too rapid both Beingness and Havingness suffer. When change is too slow both Beingness and Havingness suffer. For Change is essentially the redirection of energy.

In the assessment of a preclear one can easily trace, by use of the triangle, Be, Have and Do, and by placing this over a second triangle with space at the point of Be, time at the point of Have and energy at the point of Do, where the preclear is over-balanced and why the preclear cannot handle time or why he is trying to occupy too much space without being able to fill it, or why his life is complicated with too much havingness and has reduced his beingness to nought.

In the MEST universe as well as in a constructed universe, these three factors should be balanced for orderly progress.

103

Creative Processing

The whole of the data covered in this volume is utilized in creative processing. When one has mastered the component parts of the mind and the inter-relationships of space, energy, items and experience, he will find creative processing surprisingly easy to apply and productive of very swift results. The goal of this process is the rehabilitation of as much of the thetan's capability as possible to permit him to utilize or be free of bodies as he chooses and, even in lesser magnitude, to rid the preclear of psycho-somatics, eradicate compulsions, obsessions and inhibitions, to raise his reaction time and intelligence level. This process does whatever has been previously intended by earlier processes—utilizing a knowledge of these in order to assess the state of the preclear, and in order to parallel this difficulty with creation, change and destruction of mock-ups.

Gradient scales are vitally necessary in the application of creative processing. The term "gradient scale" can apply to anything, and means a scale of condition graduated from zero to infinity. Absolutes are considered to be unobtainable. Depending on the direction the scale is graduated, there could be an infinity of wrongness and an infinity of rightness. Thus the gradient scale of rightness would run from the theoretical but unobtainable zero of rightness, up to the theoretical infinity of rightness. A gradient scale of wrongness would run from a zero of wrongness to an infinity of wrongness. The word "gradient" is meant to define lessening or increasing degrees of condition. The difference between one point on a graduated scale and another point could be as different or as wide as the entire range of the scale itself, or it could be so tiny as to need the most minute discernment for its establishment. The gradient scale of the creation of a being could be—but in creative processing generally is not—concerned with time. In creative processing, the gradient scale, as it would refer to the creation of a person, could be, first, the envisionment of an area where the person might have been

104

or might be; then the envisionment of an area the person commonly frequented; at last, the creation of a footprint the person had made, and then perhaps some article of apparel or a possession such as a handkerchief. The creative steps would then continue until more and more of a person was established, and at last the entire person would have been created. Likewise in the destruction of a person, the gradient scale could, but generally would not, begin with blowing him up or making him grow old. If the auditor finds the preclear diffident about destroying an illusion of some person, the environment can first be diminished slightly; then perhaps the person's shadow might be shortened, and so on until the entire person could be destroyed. The essence of gradient scale work is to do as much creation, change or destruction in terms of illusion as the preclear can accomplish with confidence, and to go from successful step to greater step until an entire success in destruction, alteration or creation (or their companion states of experience, such as start, change and stop) is accomplished.

The mind works easily if led through successive successes into a complete confidence. The mind can be confused and set back enormously by demanding that it do too much too fast. The same "too much" can be accomplished by requesting of the mind that it do small portions of the task; this does not mean that processing should go slowly or that illusions which are easy to create, change or destroy should have much time spent on them. It does mean that as soon as an auditor has established a disability on the part of the preclear in creating illusions of certain places, persons, conditions, things, colours or any other thing in this or any other universe, he approaches the subject gradually by gradient scale and by accomplishing repeated successes with the preclear of greater and greater magnitude, finally achieving a complete ba.iishment of the disability.

The reason a preclear cannot alter a postulate, or change or start or stop, lies in the influence upon him of his agreements and experiences in the MEST and other universes.

To run out these agreements and experiences as such would be, in part, to agree with them over again. The mind is actually quite free to alter postulates and change its own condition, if permitted to do so at a speed that it finds comfortable. The mind will not take wide divergences which seem to it to tend toward its own diminishment or destruction. It was by a gradient scale of agreement that he came at last to accept and very nearly succumb to the MEST universe itself. The build-up of illusion was so slow and insidious that only the closest assessment would reveal to the preclear and the auditor how far these tiny steps of agreement led at last.

The motto of the MEST universe could be said to be: "Thou shalt have no force nor illusion, nor thine own space, nor self-made energy or thing, for all illusion is mine and with that thou shalt agree. If thou art, I shall not be." By a series of minute agreements, the preclear has at last given up all his own belief in his ability to make a universe, or even to create and maintain minor illusions. He does not know or even suspect that he is capable of producing illusions sufficiently strong to be observable by others, and if he thought this were true, he would attribute it to some mysterious thing and, so short and final are the punishments of the MEST universe, he would tend to shy away from this; but upon his ability to create illusion depends the very existence of all his hopes and dreams and any beauty he will ever see or feel. In truth, all sensation which he believes to come from these masses of illusory energy known as the MEST universe, are first implanted through agreement upon what he is to perceive and then perceived again by himself, with the step hidden that he has extended his own sensation to be felt and perceived by himself. He is fully convinced that the MEST universe itself has sensation which it can deliver to him, whereas all the MEST universe has is an enforced agreement which though of no substance, yet by a gradient scale came to be an illusion which seems very masterful to a preclear. To prove the reality and solidity of the MEST universe, the preclear could pound his fist upon a desk and demonstrate that his fist had met something. He is making again the error of implanting sensation and not knowing he has implanted it, for the fist which he pounds on the desk is a MEST universe fist consisting of MEST universe energy, which is itself a MEST universe agreement, and it is meeting a desk which is MEST universe; he is only demonstrating that when the MEST universe is perceived to impact upon the MEST universe, one can then implant a realistic impact and perceive it for his own wonderful edification. Reality, then, is a delusion because it is one's own illusion which has been disowned by one and is then received by one as being another thing. Only by shedding all responsibility for one's own energy can one fall into this covert trap. If one is unwilling to be responsible for energy, he is capable of using energy and then not perceiving that he uses it. One who blames others continually can be discovered to effect most of the things for which he is blaming other people. In such a way, an individual with the "very best MEST universe, Mark 10,000 ears" takes no responsibility for having implanted the sensation of sound in order to receive the sensation of sound. A preclear as he comes up the tone-scale more and more often catches himself doing this, and even though he does not know the principles involved (for no preclear has to be educated in Scientology to receive benefit from it), he recognizes that even in the case of a loud crash, his continuation of association from his environment permits him to perceive with others that a crash has taken place of objects which he with others continuously re-creates solidly, and that he must actually cause for his own perception the sound of the crash. In that the beingness of an individual is actually extended for miles in all directions around him, if not much further, any idea or thought or past thought (as there is no past) is part of his beingness, and so he must continually strive to be "faithful to his agreements with the MEST universe."

To undo this state of affairs it is only necessary to rehabilitate the awareness of the preclear that he himself is capable of creating illusions. As he rehabilitates this faculty, the preclear, without any coaching or evaluation on the part of the auditor, begins to recognize that his viewpoint is expanding and that he is becoming all-pervasive, but that he can collect his awareness at any point, and that the "brutal reality" all around him is continuously manufactured by himself out of agreements and association with other viewpoints. So long as he is fixed in a condition where he is in agreement with all spaces and viewpoints, he sees and feels automatically with all other such viewpoints. He is above the level of energy, if one can use the term, on the same wavelength with all other beingness, a condition which does not permit differentiation. As he rehabilitates his abilities in independent creation, he can change this "wavelength" at will, and can go into or out of agreement with all other points of beingness. The matter of perceiving, then, becomes entirely a matter of self-choice. It is, for instance, quite startling to a preclear to discover that as soon as he is free of the ridges of the body (which is to say, when he has discovered he can change his viewpoint) that he is already partly out of agreement with other viewpoints, and that the MEST universe becomes slightly jumbled. He is apt to be very anxious about this, for it is in conflict with the agreements to which he is subject. He immediately may struggle very hard to regain a state of affairs whereby he can view the MEST universe as everyone else views it. Indeed, the auditor must continually be on guard to prevent the preclear from attempting to re-assume these agreements. A badly-trained auditor can always be identified by the fact that he shares the preclear's anxiety that the preclear view the environment as the environment "should be." The reason why a non-cleared auditor does not do well with these processes is that he is very anxious for the preclear to continue agreement with all others and to perceive the surroundings as exactly when exteriorized as he did when he was looking through MEST eyes and perceptions (which is to say, when the preclear was at his exact, agreed-upon point of viewpoint). The ability to perceive the MEST universe is the ability to agree. The preclear's accuracy of perception of the MEST universe is of no consequence. An auditor can act to permit or even encourage a preclear to try to see, feel and hear the MEST universe when exteriorized long before the preclear is prepared to do so with equanimity. The auditor when doing this, is dramatizing his own urge to agree with viewpoints and perceive. A preclear who exteriorizes readily may find with a shock that he is not perceiving the MEST universe as he commonly supposes it should be perceived and quickly go back into his body to reassure himself that he is "keeping his contract of agreement." If the auditor demands that the preclear perceive the environment when exteriorized, then the auditor will discover that the preclear will drop in tone and that, when he has gone into his body once more, a great deal of patient auditing is necessary to regain the preclear's confidence in himself. The preclear exteriorizing may find himself in all sorts of space and time cross-ups, for he has insufficient command of space and energy to independently sort out viewpoints when unassisted by the orientation of the MEST body itself, which is, of course, in debased and degraded agreement of a very set nature.

There are two "shuns." These are invalidation and evaluation. The auditor must eschew them vigorously. The major invalidation which could be practised in using Scientology 8–8008 would be a demand that the preclear see the environment as it is seen through MEST perception or to criticize him for not being able to do so. The majority of the preclear's perceptions may be correct but some percentage of his perception is going to be enough "off wavelength" with other agreement viewpoints to cause him to perceive strangely. After a very large amount of auditing, when the preclear has regained his ability to create with considerable solidity his own illusions, it will be found that the preclear can at will perceive the MEST universe and can do so with accuracy. He can further, without the aid of a body, move objects and do a thousand other "interesting tricks" which could very well be viewed with considerable awe, for they have not been seen on earth in recorded history but have lived in legend.

Using Standard Operating Procedure, Issue 3, as given in this volume, the auditor yet takes a very thorough assessment of his preclear with an E-Meter. He discovers, in accordance with information in this book, what the preclear is unable to start, change, stop; create, alter, destroy; be, do or have; differentiate, associate or identify; on each and every one of the eight dynamics and their component parts. The auditor makes a complete list. This is the Can't list.   Exteriorized, if possible, or interiorized as in the later numbered cases, the preclear is then made to "mock-up" illusions about each one of these Can'ts and to change the size, character and position of the illusion or any part thereof in space, shift it in time simply by knowing it has been shifted by him, until at last the preclear is able to handle the whole object of the Can't with complete facility.

Can'ts may be an inability to destroy women or snakes or specific persons, or create machinery, or write legibly. The preclear is requested to accomplish by illusions the smallest gradient of the Can't with which he can successfully start; and, under auditor direction, by moving this small portion of the whole here and there in space, tipping it this way and that and making it, in particular, disobey "natural laws" in the MEST universe, the preclear is led to an ability to create, change or destroy the Can't.

The Can't is also the Must. Can't is an inhibition; Must is an enforcement. What *must* the preclear do and what must be done to him? By whom? By creative processing and gradient scales, he achieves mock-ups until each one of these musts becomes a "Can if I want to, but don't have to."

There are also the Desires. These are the cravings for sensation or possession or identification which brought the preclear into and made him continue agreements. Behind every case the Desires are paramount and of greater importance than the Can'ts. Why does he desire bodies? Why is his second dynamic aberrated? Why does he feel he cannot be free? Can he differentiate between his own actual want-ingness and the wantingness of MEST itself which is trying to have him? The desires are resolved by creative process-ing wherein the preclear does mock-ups of the necessary acts which he desires or the necessary behaviours which brought him into agreement until he can at last laugh at them.

In that creative processing does not take long in terms of time, the assessment list can afford to be very broad and to cover every possible phase through the system of the dynamics and the cycles of action.

This is a list of things the preclear must be able to do with an illusion:

> Create the condition, energy or object
> Conserve it
> Protect it
> Control it
> Hide it
> Change it
> Age it
> Make it go backwards on a cycle of action
> Perceive it with all perceptions
> Shift it at will in time
> Rearrange it
> Duplicate it
> Turn it upside down or on the side at will
> Make it disobey MEST laws
> Be it
> Not be it
> Destroy it.

In order to accomplish these things, if the whole of any condition cannot be fulfilled by gradient scale some tiny por-tion of the condition must be fulfilled.

When a small condition has been fulfilled, the condition is then enlarged until the whole condition can be fulfilled.

That preclear who cannot get even a shadow of an illusion

so that he can perceive it in any manner must be coaxed to see white spots, black spots, of his own creation, and to change those in space and time, enlarge and contract them, until he has a certain command and control of black and white. This must be done with such a preclear without regard to the number of hours it takes or the patience of the drill. It can be done with the eyes open or closed, whichever the preclear finds best.

When the preclear is discovered to be trying to prevent a motion or condition, the auditor should magnify that very condition with new mock-ups related to it, i.e., if objects keep rushing in on the preclear, mock up objects rushing in until the action is enormously magnified but under the preclear's complete control. If the preclear cannot start something, make him stop it. If he cannot reverse a direction, make him change the nature of the object which he is trying to reverse enough times to permit him to reverse the original disability. If the preclear cannot create something, have him create anything even vaguely associated with it, and by association at last have him mock up the actual thing.

The essence of creative processing is moving objects in space when they have been mocked up. They are moved near and far, to the right, left, behind the preclear, below his feet, above his head and in front of him. He must *know* that he has changed the location of the object. If he cannot make a large change, have him do a small change of location. If he cannot do a small change of location, have him alter the object by turning it different colours, or by enlarging or contracting it, or by pushing it away or bringing it near him, until he can make it move sideways. In failing to do this, have him do a change with some allied object.

The essence of creative processing is a continuation of success. Be careful not to give the preclear things which make him fail. Do not let his failures mount up. Estimate the preclear and pay attention to what he is doing; find out from him continually the condition of his illusions, if you yourself as an auditor cannot see them. Putting objects into

112

yesterday or tomorrow or well into the future or into the past is vitally necessary to processing.

Control of the illusion is the essence of commands. The preclear must be able to create, grow, conserve, decay and destroy; start, change and stop; be, do and have; differentiate, associate and identify; handle in space, with energy and in time, any object, actual or mythical, in all the eight dynamics, and with high preference given to anything which disobeys "natural laws" of the MEST universe.

That auditor with a high order of imagination who is himself clear, finds mock-ups very easy to "think up" and request of the preclear, but it is not necessary to have such an imagination, as a routine assessment will discover immediately that the most ordinary things fall into the Can't, Must and Desire brackets in the preclear's life.

The preclear will be discovered on the first dynamic, quite ordinarily, not to be able to create, change or destroy, especially destroy, his own body or bodies in which he thinks he is encased within his own body (old time-track bodies such as a Fifth Invader Force body). He will be found to be incapable in many directions with facsimiles, communication lines and other matters on the first dynamic alone. On the second dynamic, many incapabilities will come to view, and so on along all the dynamics. On the fifth dynamic, he will quite ordinarily be found incapable of handling snakes, spiders, vicious fish, bacteria, wild animals and domestic pets. On the seventh dynamic he will be discovered unable to handle other thetans, even in the most elementary fashion of bringing two dots of light into proximity and then separating them (an exercise which blows head ridges in many preclears quite explosively). On the eighth dynamic his limitations quite ordinarily become too obvious for comment, but on each and every dynamic he must be able to do or fulfil any of the above cycles or conditions.

Standard Operating Procedure tells how to exteriorize a thetan. Creative processing, rising-scale postulate changing, postulate processing, are then necessary to bring him toward

113

a state of a cleared theta clear. The state of theta clear simply demands that the preclear remains outside his body when the body itself is hurt, and the state is adequate to prevent his being trapped again by a body except in unusual circumstances. There is no guarantee of long continuance in the condition. The state of cleared theta clear is, however, another thing, for it means a person who is able to create his own universe; or, living in the MEST universe, is able to create illusions perceivable by others at will, to handle MEST universe objects without mechanical means and to have and feel no need of bodies or even the MEST universe to keep himself and his friends interested in existence.

STANDARD OPERATING PROCEDURE 8

The basic technology of this operating procedure is to be found in The Factors, *Scientology 8–8008* and at the Professional School.

In using this operating procedure, the auditor should give every heed to the AUDITOR'S CODE. Further, he should audit the preclear in the presence of a third person or another auditor.

This operating procedure is best done by an auditor who has been thoroughly trained in all processes involving the reduction of the past and its incidents; the untrained auditor may encounter manifestations with which only a professional auditor would be familiar.

This operating procedure retains the most workable methods of preceding procedures and, in itself, emphasizes POSITIVE GAIN and the present and future rather than negative gain of eradication of the past.

The thetan, exteriorized and rehabilitated, can handle and remedy by direct address of his own energy to the body and the removal of old energy deposits, all body malfunctions or mental aberrations attacked by older processes. The goal of this procedure is not the rehabilitation of the body but of the thetan. Rehabilitation of a body incidentally ensues.

The goal of this procedure is OPERATING THETAN, a higher goal than earlier procedures.

The auditor tests the preclear for each step from Step I on until he finds a step the preclear can do. The auditor then completes this step and then the next higher step until the thetan is exteriorized. With the thetan exteriorized, the auditor now completes all seven steps regardless of the steps performed before exteriorization. He may complete all these steps and all parts of these steps rapidly. But they must be done to obtain a theta clear and they must be done thoroughly to obtain an OPERATING THETAN.

The techniques involved herein were developed by L. Ron Hubbard and after testing by him, were tested by other auditors on a wide variety of cases. It is doubtful if any earlier process of any kind in any age has been as thoroughly validated as this operating procedure. However, it works only when used as stated. Disorganized fragments of this material, given other names and emphasis, may be found to be harmful. Irresponsible and untrained use of this procedure is not authorized. Capricious or quasi-religious exteriorization of the thetan for other purposes than the restoration of his ability and self-determinism should be resisted by any being. The goal of this process is freedom for the individual to the betterment of the many.

STEP I—Ask preclear to be three feet behind his head. If stable there, have him be in various pleasant places until any feeling of scarcity of viewpoints is resolved; then have him be in several undesirable places, then several pleasant places; then have him be in a slightly dangerous place, then in more and more dangerous places until he can sit in the center of the sun. Be sure to observe gradient scale of ugliness and dangerousness of places. Do not let preclear fail. Then do remaining steps with preclear exteriorized.

STEP II—Have preclear mock up own body. If he does this easily and clearly, have him mock up own body until he slips out of it. When he is exteriorized and knows it thoroughly (the conditions of all exteriorization) do Step I. If his mock-up was not clear, go to Step III immediately.

STEP III—SPACATION: Have preclear close his eyes and find upper corners of the room. Have him sit there, not thinking, refusing to think of anything, interested only in the corners until he is completely exteriorized without strain. Then do a spacation (constructing own space with eight

116

anchor points and holding it stable without effort) and go to Step I. If preclear was unable to locate corners of the room easily with his eyes closed, go to Step IV.

STEP IV—EXPANDED GITA: (This is an extension of "Give and Take" processing.) Test preclear to see if he can get a mock-up he can see, no matter how vague. Then have him WASTE, ACCEPT UNDER DURESS, DESIRE and finally be able to TAKE OR LEAVE ALONE each of the items listed below. He does this with mock-ups or ideas. He must do the sequence of WASTE, etc., in the order given here for each item. He wastes it by having it at remote distances in places where it will do no good, being used or done or observed by something which cannot appreciate it; when he is able to waste it in vast quantities the auditor then has him accept it in mock-up form until he no longer is antagonistic to having to accept it even when it is unpleasant and great force is applied to make him take it; then, again with mock-ups, he must be able to bring himself to desire it even in its worst form; then, by mock-ups of it in its most desirable form he must come to be able to leave it entirely alone or take it in its worst form without caring. EXPANDED GITA remedies contra-survival abundance and scarcity. It will be found that before one can accept a very scarce (to him) thing, he has to give it away. A person with a milk allergy must be able to give away, in mock-up, enormous quantities of milk, wasting it, before he can accept any himself. The items in this list are compounded from several years of isolating what factors were more important to minds than others; the list lacks very few of the very important items if any; additions to or subtractions from this list should not be attempted. *Viewpoint, work* and *pain* should be heavily and often stressed and given priority.

WASTE, HAVE FORCED UPON, DESIRE, BE ABLE TO GIVE OR TAKE, IN THAT ORDER, EACH OF THE FOLLOWING: (Order of items here is random).

117

VIEWPOINT, WORK, PAIN, BEAUTY, MOTION, ENGRAMS, UGLINESS, LOGIC, PICTURES, CONFINEMENT, MONEY, PARENTS, BLACKNESS, POLICE, LIGHT, EXPLOSIONS, BODIES, DEGRADATION, MALE BODIES, FEMALE BODIES, BABIES, CHILDREN MALE, CHILDREN FEMALE, STRANGE AND PECULIAR BODIES, DEAD BODIES, AFFINITY (LOVE), AGREEMENT, BEAUTIFUL BODIES, PEOPLE, ATTENTION, ADMIRATION, FORCE, ENERGY, LIGHTNING, UNCONSCIOUSNESS, PROBLEMS, ANTAGONISM, REVERENCE, FEAR, OBJECTS, TIME, EATING HUMAN BODIES, SOUND, GRIEF, BEAUTIFUL SADNESS, HIDDEN INFLUENCES, HIDDEN COMMUNICATIONS, DOUBTS, FACES, DIMENSION POINTS, ANGER, APATHY, IDEAS, ENTHUSIASM, DISAGREEMENT, HATE, SEX, REWARD, EATING PARENTS, EATEN BY MOTHER, EATEN BY FATHER, EATING MEN, EATEN BY MEN, EATING WOMEN, EATEN BY WOMEN, START, BROKEN COMMUNICATIONS, WRITTEN COMMUNICATIONS, STILLNESS, EXHAUSTION, WOMEN STOPPING MOTION, MEN STOPPING MOTION, CHANGING MOTION WOMEN, CHANGING MOTION MEN, CHANGING MOTION BABIES, CHANGING MOTION CHILDREN, STARTING MOTION MEN, STARTING MOTION WOMEN, STARTING MOTION CHILDREN, STARTING MOTION OBJECTS, STARTING MOTION SELF, OMENS, WICKEDNESS, FORGIVENESS, PLAY, GAMES, SOUND, MACHINERY, TOUCH, TRAFFIC, STOLEN GOODS, STOLEN PICTURES, HOMES, BLASPHEMY, CAVES, MEDICINE, GLASS, MIRRORS, PRIDE, MUSICAL INSTRUMENTS, DIRTY WORDS, SPACE, WILD ANIMALS, PETS, BIRDS, AIR, WATER, FOOD, MILK, GARBAGE, GASES, EXCRETA, ROOMS, BEDS, PUNISHMENT, BOREDOM, CONFUSION, SOLDIERS, EXECUTIONERS, DOCTORS, JUDGES, PSYCHIATRISTS, ALCOHOLIC LIQUOR, DRUGS,

118

MASTURBATION, REWARDS, HEAT, COLD, FORBID-
DEN THINGS, GOD, THE DEVIL, SPIRITS, BACTERIA,
GLORY, DEPENDENCE, RESPONSIBILITY, WRONG-
NESS, RIGHTNESS, INSANITY, SANITY, FAITH,
CHRIST, DEATH, RANK, POVERTY, MAPS, IRRE-
SPONSIBILITY, GREETINGS, FAREWELLS, CREDIT,
LONELINESS, JEWELS, TEETH, GENITALIA, COM-
PLICATIONS, HELP, PRETENCE, TRUTH, LIES,
ASSURANCE, CONTEMPT, PREDICTABILITY, UN-
PREDICTABILITY, VACUUMS, WHITE CLOUDS,
BLACK CLOUDS, UNATTAINABLES, HIDDEN
THINGS, WORRY, REVENGE, TEXTBOOKS, KISSES,
THE PAST, THE FUTURE, THE PRESENT, ARMS,
STOMACHS, BOWELS, MOUTHS, CIGARETTES,
SMOKE, URINE, VOMIT, CONVULSIONS, SALIVA,
FLOWERS, SEMEN, BLACKBOARDS, FIREWORKS,
TOYS, VEHICLES, DOLLS, AUDIENCES, DOORS,
WALLS, WEAPONS, BLOOD, AMBITIONS, ILLUSIONS,
BETRAYAL, RIDICULE, HOPE, HAPPINESS,
MOTHERS, FATHERS, GRANDPARENTS, SUNS,
PLANETS, MOONS, SENSATION, LOOKING, INCI-
DENTS, WAITING, SILENCE, TALKING, KNOWING,
NOT KNOWING, DOUBTS, FAC ONE, REMEMBER-
ING, FORGETTING, AUDITING, MINDS, FAME,
POWER, ACCIDENTS, ILLNESSES, APPROVAL,
TIREDNESS, FACES, ACTING, DRAMA, COSTUMES,
SLEEP, HOLDING THINGS APART, HOLDING
THINGS TOGETHER, DESTROYING THINGS, SEND-
ING THINGS AWAY, MAKING THINGS GO FAST,
MAKING THINGS APPEAR, MAKING THINGS VANISH,
CONVICTIONS, STABILITY, CHANGING PEOPLE,
SILENT MEN, SILENT WOMEN, SILENT CHILDREN,
SYMBOLS OF WEAKNESS, SYMBOLS OF FORCE, DIS-
ABILITIES, EDUCATION, LANGUAGES, BESTIALITY,
HOMOSEXUALITY, INVISIBLE BODIES, INVISIBLE
ACTS, INVISIBLE SCENES, ACCEPTING THINGS
BACK, GAMES, RULES, PLAYERS, RESTIMULATION,

119

SEXUAL RESTIMULATION, SPACE REDUCTION, SIZE REDUCTION, ENTERTAINMENT, CHEERFULNESS, FREEDOM FOR OTHERS TO TALK, ACT, FEEL PAIN, BE SAD, THETANS, PERSONALITIES, CRUELTY, ORGANIZATIONS.

WARNING: SHOULD YOUR PRECLEAR BECOME UNSTABLE OR UPSET DOING THIS PROCESS TAKE HIM TO STEP VI, THEN RETURN TO THIS LIST.

COMMENT: The mind is sufficiently complicated that it can be expected to have computations on almost all the above. Thus there is no single clearing button and search for it is at the dictate of a circuit, the mechanism of circuits being to search for something hidden. Thus your preclear may begin to compute and philosophize and seek to find the "button" that will release all this. All this releases all the buttons so tell him to relax and go on with the process every time he starts to compute.

NOTE: Running the above will bring to the surface without further attention the "computation on the case" and the service facsimile. Do not audit these. Run Expanded Gita.

STEP V—PRESENT TIME DIFFERENTIATION. EXTERIORIZATION BY SCENERY. Have preclear, with his body's eyes, study and see the difference between similar real objects such as the two legs of a chair, the spaces between the back, two cigarettes, two trees, two girls. He must see and study the objects, it is not enough to remember objects. The definition of a CASE V is "no mock-ups, only blackness." Have him continue this process until he is alert. Use liberally and often.

Then exteriorize by having the preclear close his eyes and move actual places on Earth under him, preferably places he has not been. Have him bring these up to him, find two similar things in the scene and observe the difference between them. Move him over oceans and cities until he is certain that he is exteriorized.

Then, preferably while exteriorized, have him do STEP I.

120

This case has to know before he can be. His viewpoint is in the past. Give him present time viewpoints until he is a STEP I by the methods given for STEP V.

(COMMENT: PRESENT TIME DIFFERENTIATION is a very good general technique and resolves chronic somatics and improves tone.)

STEP VI—A-R-C STRAIGHT WIRE using next to last list of SELF ANALYSIS IN SCIENTOLOGY which asks preclear to recall something really real to him, etc. Then use the lists in SELF ANALYSIS. This level is the neurotic level. It is identified by the preclear having mock-ups which will not persist or which won't go away. Use also PRESENT TIME DIFFERENTIATION. Then go to STEP IV. At any drop in tone, return case to STEP VI.

STEP VII—PSYCHOTIC CASES.* Whether in or out of body, the psychotic looks to be in such desperate straits that people often err in thinking desperate measures are necessary. Use the lightest possible methods. Give case space and freedom where possible. Have psychotic IMITATE (not mock up) various things. Have him do PRESENT TIME DIFFERENTIATION. Get him to tell the difference between things by actual touch. Have him locate, differentiate and touch things that are really real to him (real objects or items). If inaccessible mimic him with own body whatever he does until he comes into communication. Have him locate corners of the room and hold them without thinking. As soon as his communication is up, go to STEP VI but be very sure he changes any mock-up around until he knows it is a mock-up, that it exists and that he himself made it. Do not run engrams. He is psychotic because viewpoints in present time are so scarce that he has gone into the past for viewpoints which at least he knew existed. By

---

* It is not the purpose of Scientology to handle psychotics, but rather to "make the able more able". The above is included, however, as valuable data for the handling of psychotics.

PRESENT TIME DIFFERENTIATION, by tactile on objects, return his idea of an abundance of viewpoint in present time. If he has been given electric shock, do not process it or any other brutality. Work him for very brief periods for his attention span is short. *Always* work psychotics with another person or a companion present.

NOTE: ALL STEPS FOR ALL CASES. IF IN DOUBT AS TO CONDITION OF CASE, TEST WITH STEP VI.

NOTE: An Operating Thetan must also be able to manufacture particles of admiration and force in abundance.

STEP I—The Operating Thetan must be able to manufacture and experience to his complete satisfaction all sensations including pain in mock-up form and all energies such as admiration and force. It will be found that some STEP I cases will not be able to manufacture admiration particles.

STEP II—Be very careful not to make a lower step preclear, while still in a body, mock up his own body too long. Any mock-up will appear if it is simply put there often enough and long enough—providing the preclear doesn't spin in the process. The long term manufacture of mock-ups of one's own body and of admiration may not produce quite the results expected—communication lines which should remain shut may open with bad results. These lines that are shut appear like hard, black cords to the preclear.

There are two types of techniques in general: POSITIVE GAIN and NEGATIVE GAIN as defined in the above text. POSITIVE CAN BE ADMINISTERED IN UNLIMITED AMOUNTS WITHOUT HARM. Negative gain techniques such as the reduction of engrams and locks double-terminalling, black and white, are often limited in the length of time they can be given: after a few hundred hours of early type auditing the case could be found to slump. Thus we have in POSITIVE GAIN the unlimited technique which improves the analytical mind; in NEGATIVE GAIN we have a *limited* (in terms of the time it can be audited) technique. In SOP 8 the following steps and processes may be audited without limit: STEP I, STEP III, STEP V, STEP VI, STEP VII.

The following steps are limited and should not be audited many hours without changing to another type (unlimited for a while, after which the following steps could be resumed): STEP II, STEP IV.

THE FOLLOWING STEPS CAN BE USED ON GROUPS: Step III, Step V, part 1 and part 2, Step VI, Step VII.

The following is a list of effective procedures as of April 28th, 1953. If a procedure is labelled (U) it is unlimited and could be audited thousands of hours and only improve a case: if labelled (L) it is limited and must be handled with discretion and alternated with an unlimited technique: if it is labelled (S) it is seldom used: if labelled (A) it is used in assists.

    Engram Running, Book One (L) (A)
* Grief and Other Secondaries (L) (A)
    Lock Scanning (L) (A)
    Emotional Curves (L) (S)
    Service Facsimile Chain as Engrams (L) (S)
    Effort Processing (L) (A)
    ARC Straight Wire, Science of Survival (A)
    Negative Exteriorization (L)
    Ridge Running (L)
* Ded-Dedex (L) (S) (Current lifetime used for fast releases)
    Motivator-Overt (L) (S)
    Matched Terminals in Mock-ups (L) (S)
    Double Terminals in Mock-ups (L) (A)
* Positive Exteriorization (Step I SOP 8) (U)
* Own Body Mock-up (Step II SOP 8) (L)
* Spacation (Step III SOP 8 and General Usage) (U)
* Expanded Gita (Step IV SOP 8) (L)
* Present Time Differentiation (Step V SOP 8) (U)
* Exteriorization by Scenery (Step V SOP 8) (U)

* Self Analysis in Scientology and British S.A. in Dianetics
  (same volume) (Step VI SOP 8) (U)
* Imitation of Things (Step VII SOP 8) (U)
* Creative Processing (as in Scientology 8–8008) (U)

The symbol (*) before a process above means it is recommended.

ADDITIONAL NOTE ON EXPANDED GITA: The governing rule here is that the preclear craves exactly what he has and must waste whatever he doesn't have. It is better, in the opinion of a thetan, to have anything no matter how "bad" rather than have nothing. He craves those things which are scarce but he can't even have those things which are scarcest. In order to have what he cannot have he first must be able to waste it (in mock-up) in quantity. An abbreviated form of this process would involve, over and over, wasting, accepting under duress, the following items in turn:

TRY FIRST: *HEALTHY BODIES, STRONG BODIES, GOOD PERCEPTION, GOOD RECALL, VIEWPOINTS, PAIN, WORK, FREEDOM FOR OTHERS TO HAVE VIEWPOINTS.*

The preclear cannot be free himself until he has freed others. This does not work out in the MEST universe but it works out in mock-ups.

CIRCUITS GO INTO ACTION ON MANY OF THESE PROCESSES: DON'T PERMIT YOUR PRECLEAR TO THINK, DON'T BE INTERESTED IN WHAT HE THINKS. FAILURE TO FOLLOW THIS RULE WILL CAUSE THE PROCESS TO FAIL.

COMPARISON OF MEST OBJECTS TO MOCK-UPS RESOLVES WHY THETANS MAKE FACSIMILES AND DISCLOSES TO THE PRECLEAR THE MECHANISM. THIS IS A GOOD PROCESS AND CAN BE DONE AT STEP IV AS AN ADDITIONAL PART OF IV. HAVE PRECLEAR MAKE A MOCK-UP THE SAME AS A MEST OBJECT AND PUT THE MOCK-UP ALONGSIDE

OF THE MEST OBJECT AND THEN COMPARE THEM. THE MOCK-UPS WILL GRADUALLY IM-PROVE, THEN KEY OUT THE MECHANISM THAT MAKES FACSIMILES.

CERTAINTY PROCESSING

SOP–8 Appendix No. 2

The anatomy of maybe consists of uncertainties and is resolved by the processing of certainties. It is not resolved by the processing of uncertainties.

An uncertainty is held in suspense solely because the preclear is holding on so hard to certainties. The basic thing he is holding on to is *"I have a solution," "I have no solution."* One of these is positive, the other is negative. A complete positive and a complete negative are alike a certainty. The basic certainty is *"There is something," "There is nothing."* A person can be certain there is something, he can be certain there is nothing.

"There is something," "There is nothing" resolves chronic somatics in this order. One gets the preclear to have the centre of the somatic say *"There is something here," "There is nothing here."* Then he gets the centre of the somatic to say *"There is nothing there," "There is something there."* Then the auditor has the preclear toward the somatic say *"There is something there," "There is nothing there."* And then he gets the preclear to say about himself *"There is something here," "There is nothing here."* This is a very fast resolution of chronic somatics; quite ordinarily three or four minutes of this will resolve an acute state and fifteen or twenty minutes of it will resolve a chronic state.

This matter of certainties goes further. It has been determined by my investigations that the reason behind what is happening is the desire of a cause to bring about an effect. Something is better than nothing, anything is better than nothing. Any circuit, any effect, any anything, is better than nothing. If you will match terminals in brackets *"There is nothing,"* you will find that a lot of your preclears become very ill. This should be turned around into *"There is something."*

The way one does Matched Terminals is to have the preclear facing the preclear or his father facing his father; in other words, two of each of anything, one facing the other. These two things will discharge one into the other, thus running off the difficulty. By bracket we mean, of course, running this with the preclear putting them up as himself to himself as though they were put up by somebody else, the somebody else facing the somebody else, and the matched terminal again put up by others facing others.

The clue to all this is positive and negative in terms of certainties. The positive plus the negative in conflict make an uncertainty. A great number of combinations of things can be run. Here's a list of the combinations: —

The button behind sex is *"I can begin life anew," "I cannot begin life anew," "I can make life persist," "I cannot make life persist," "I can stop life," "I cannot stop life," "I can change life," "I cannot change life," "I can start life," "I cannot start life."*

A very effective process, *"Something wrong . . . ," "Nothing wrong . . ."* with *"you me, they, my mind, communications, various allies."*

A very basic resolution of the lack of space of an individual is to locate those people and those objects which you've been using as anchor points such as father, mother and so forth and putting them into matched terminal brackets with this: —*"There is father," "There is no father," "There is grandfather," "There is no grandfather."* In the compulsive line this can be changed to *"There must be no father," "There must be a father."* One takes all the allies of an individual and runs them in this fashion.

The basic law underneath this is that a person becomes the effect of anything upon which he has had to depend. This would tell you immediately that the sixth dynamic, the MEST universe, is the largest dependency of the individual. This can be run out, but then any dynamic can be run out in this fashion. *"There is myself," "There is no self,"* and so on up the dynamics. *"(Any dynamic) is preventing me from communicating," "(Any dynamic) is not preventing me from communicating"* is intensely effective. Any such technique can be varied by applying the sub-zero scale as found earlier in this book.

One runs any certainty out because he knows that for this certainly there is an opposite negative certainty and that between these lies a maybe, and that the maybe is suspense in time. The basic operation of the reactive mind is to solve problems. It is based on uncertainties about observation. Thus one runs out certainties of observation. The most general shotgun technique would have to do with *"There is sex," "There is no sex," "There is force," "There is no force."* This could be run, of course, in terms of matched terminal brackets or even as concepts, but one must not neglect to run the overt act phenomenon which is to say getting somebody else getting the concept.

The processing out of certainties would then embrace *"I have a solution," "There is no solution."* These two opposite ends would take care of any individual who was hung on the track with some solution, for that solution had its opposite. People who have studied medicine begin by being certain that medicine works and end by being certain that medicine doesn't work. They begin by studying psychology on a supposition that it is the solution, and finish up that it is not the solution. This also happens to superficial students of Dianetics and Scientology, thus one should also run *"Dianetics is a solution," "Dianetics is not the solution."* This would also get one off the maybe on the subject.

We are essentially processing communications systems. The entire process of auditing is concentrated upon withdrawing communications from the preclear as predicated on the basis of the body and the preclear cannot handle communications. Thus *"The preclear can handle communications," "The preclear cannot handle communications"* is a shotgun technique which resolves maybes about his communications.

An intensely interesting aspect of Certainty Processing is that it shows up intimately where the preclear is aberrated. Here is the overall basic technique. One runs *"There is ...," "There is not ..."* the following: *Communication, talk, letters, love, agreement, sex, pain, work, bodies, minds, curiosity, control, enforcement, compulsion, inhibition, food, money, people, ability, beauty, ugliness, presents* and both the top and bottom of the Chart of Attitudes, positive and negative in each one.

Basic in all this is the urge of the preclear to produce an effect, so one can run *"I can produce an effect upon mama," "I cannot produce an effect upon mama,"* and so forth for all allies and one will resolve the fixations of attention on the part of the preclear. Thus fixations of attention are resolved by Certainty Processing, processing out the production of effect.

One can occasionally, if he so desires, process the direct centre of the maybe, which is to say doubt itself, in terms of Matched Terminals. This, however, is risky for it throws the preclear into a general state of doubt.

The key to any such processing is the recovery of viewpoints. *"I can have grandfather's viewpoint," "I cannot have grandfather's viewpoint,"* and so on, particularly with sexual partners, will prove intensely interesting on a case. *"There are viewpoints," "There are no viewpoints," "I have a viewpoint," "I don't have a viewpoint," "Blank has a viewpoint," "Blank has no viewpoint,"* resolves problems.

One should also realize that when one is processing facsimiles, he is processing at once energy, sensation and aesthetics. The facsimile is a picture. The preclear is being affected by pictures mainly, and so *"There are no pictures," "There are pictures,"* forwards the case toward handling pictures; which is to say facsimiles.

A person tends to ally himself with somebody whom he considers capable of producing greater effects than himself, so *"I, she, he, it can create greater effects," "I, she, he, it can create no effect,"* is quite effective.

When one is processing, he is trying to withdraw communications. Reach and Withdraw are the two fundamentals in the action of theta. Must Reach and Cannot Reach, Must Withdraw and Cannot Withdraw are compulsions which, when run in combination, produce the manifestation of insanity in a preclear.

"I can reach," "I can't reach," "I can withdraw," "I can't withdraw," open up into the fact that remembering and forgetting are dependent upon the ability to reach and withdraw. You will find that a preclear will respond to *"You must"* or *"You can," "You must not," "You cannot," "There is," "There is not,"* forgetting and remembering.

The only reason a person is hanging on to a body or facsimile is because he has lost his belief in his ability to create. The rehabilitation of this ability to create is resolved —for instance, in a person who has had an ambition to write with *"I can write," "I cannot write"*—and so forth. The loss of this creative ability made the person hang on to what he had. The fact that a preclear has forgotten how to or no longer can himself generate force makes him hold on to stores of force. These are very often mistaken by the auditor for facsimiles. The preclear doesn't care for the facsimile, he simply cares for the force contained in the facsimile because he knows he doesn't have any force any more.

It should be kept in mind that reaching and withdrawing are intensely productive of reaction in a preclear. But that preclear who does not respond to reaching and withdrawing and certainty thereon, is hung up in a very special condition: he is trying to prevent something from happening, he is trying to maintain control. If he prevents something from happening, he also prevents auditing from happening. He has lost allies, he has had accidents, and he is hung up at all those points on the track where he feels he should have prevented something from happening. This is resolved by running *"I must prevent it from happening," "I cannot prevent it from happening." "I must retain control," "I must lose all control."*

Blackness is the desire to be an effect and the inability to be cause.

"I can create grandfather (or ally)," "I cannot create grandfather (or ally)," solves scarcity of allies. *"I want to be aware," "I want no awareness,"* is a technique which is basic in attitudes. Run this as others, in matched terminal brackets or in Expanded GITA.

Certainty there is a past, certainty there is no past; certainty there is a future, certainty there is no future; certainty it means something else, certainty it does not mean anything else; certainty there is space, certainty there is no space; certainty there is energy, certainty there is no energy; certainty there are objects, certainty there are no objects.

GLOSSARY

THETAN: This term designates the beingness of the individual, the awareness of awareness unit, that quantity and identity which IS the preclear. One does not speak of "my thetan" any more than he would speak of "my me." Persons referring to the thetan in such a way as to make the thetan a third party to the body and the person are not only incorrect, they betoken by this a bad state of aberration.

AUDITOR: The person who "audits," who computes and listens, a practitioner of Dianetics and Scientology. SOP Theta Clearing is best done by an auditor who has been theta cleared. A Step V commonly acts to force the preclear to stay in his body even while pretending to free the preclear from his body.

LOCATION: The thetan is an energy unit which is commonly located in the centre of the skull. A thetan who cannot leave the current body very often believes himself to be holding on only to the current body, and yet in actuality is holding on to a facsimile of an earlier body. The thetan also believes himself to be the size of some earlier body. A thetan from the Fifth Invader Force believes himself to be a very strange insect-like creature with unthinkably horrible hands. He believes himself to be occupying such a body, but is in actuality simply a unit capable of producing space, time, energy and matter.

SELF-DETERMINISM: Self-determinism is a relative state of ability to determine location in time and space, and to create and destroy space, time, energy and matter. If one can locate his facsimiles and ridges in time and space, if one is able to place persons and objects in the past, present and future in time and space, he can be considered to have high self-determinism. If one's facsimiles place him in time and space, if people can easily place one in time and space in the past,

132

present or future, one's self-determinism is low. Willingness and unwillingness to locate things in time and space are the key relative states of sanity.

ILLUSION: Any idea, space, energy, object or time concept which one creates himself.

REALITY: That agreement upon illusion which became the MEST universe.

DELUSION: Things not of one's own creation or of the MEST universe which locate one in time and space.

CERTAINTY: One is certain on a plus or minus basis and can be equally certain on either. One can be certain a thing is NOT real or he can be certain that it IS real. There are three sides to this. One is certain that a thing is his own illusion: this is the highest level. One is certain that a thing is a MEST universe reality (illusion). One can be certain that a thing is a delusion. Any certainty is a knowingness. Knowingness is sanity. Thus we have three routes of certainty by which to approach knowingness.

KNOWINGNESS: Knowingness depends upon certainty.

ABERRATION: Aberration depends upon uncertainty.

THETA PERCEPTION: That which one perceives by radiating toward an object and from the reflection perceiving various characteristics of the object such as size, odour, tactile, sound, colour, etc. Certainty of perception is increased by drilling in certainties as above. Theta perception is dependent upon willingness to handle energy and to create space, energy and objects. In view of the fact that the MEST universe can be established easily to be an illusion, one must have an ability to perceive illusions before one can clearly perceive the MEST universe. The thetan who cannot perceive the MEST universe easily will also be found to be incapable of handling and orienting other kinds of illusions with certainty. Theta perception is also a direct index to responsibility, for responsibility is the willingness to handle force.

133

MEST PERCEPTION: Recordings the thetan takes from the organs of perception of the human body as a short cut to perception (lazy perception). The body records actual wave emanations from the MEST universe, the thetan uses these recordings. Considerably more data should be collected on this subject.

ORIENTATION: Determination of location in space and time and determination of energy quantity present. This applies to past, present, future.

RIDGES: "Solid" accumulations of energy which are suspended in space and time. Ridges can be handled variously. They can also explode.

FACSIMILES: Energy reproductions of things in various universes. They are fixed to ridges.

END OF TERMINAL: A communication line to anything has the preclear at one end and something at the other end. When the end of terminal is vacated, flow dams and the preclear must fix the vacated end to his own body. This is the mechanics behind the loss which brings about grief. ARC lines can be mocked-up and handled in the routine of creative processing, which processes will resolve end of terminal difficulties. These terminals are quite visible to the thetan who sees them either wound around the body or extending to other bodies or reaching a considerable distance into space. The thetan can actually yank on these terminals, even those which go into space, and free the other end whether he perceives it or not, and so recover and dispose of such lines.

ASTRAL BODIES: Somebody's delusion. Astral bodies are usually mock-ups which the mystic then tries to believe real. He sees the astral body as something else and then seeks to inhabit it in the most common practices of "astral walking." Anyone who confuses astral bodies with thetans is apt to have difficulty with theta clearing for the two things are not the same order of similarity. The exteriorization of a thetan, when actually accomplished, is so complete and thorough and is attended by so many other phenomena, that anyone who has made an effort to relate these two things is quite certain to recant after he has been theta cleared. The most note worthy difference is that the thetan does not have a body. Production of illusion to which he then sought to assign MEST reality is probably the underlying factor which makes mysticism so aberrative. Data from India, even that found in the deepest "mysteries" of India, is knowingly or unknow-ingly "booby-trapped" so that while it contains, though un-evaluated and isolated, many essential truths, it contains as well directions which are certain to send the experimenter even more deeply into the unwanted state of becoming MEST. Until recently, the nearest one could come to studying the actuality of existence was through the field of mysticism and its value should not be discounted, but its effect is to deliver an entirely opposite result to any experimenter luckless enough to hope to reach cause by becoming an effect as required in mysticism. Seeing and feeling "non-existences" is frightening and harmful only when one seeks to believe them to be existences. Only when he knows he has created them, can he obtain a certainty upon them. One can create hallucination for himself only by insisting that what he has created was otherwise created—in short, refusing to accept responsibility for his own created illusions.

ELECTRONICS: Lower and cruder manifestations of the same order of actuality as thought.

TERMINALS: In facsimiles, ridges and electric motors, terminals operate and current flows only when they are fixed in time and space. Alternating current becomes possible only because of an overlooked item, the base of the motor, which is fixed in time and space and which keeps the ter-minals apart by fixing them in time and space.

THE HUMAN SOUL: The preclear.

MYSTICISM: Many right ideas but the wrong way to go about it.

135

FREEDOM: Ability to create and position energy or matter in time and space.

SLAVERY: Being positioned in another's time and space.

THE HUMAN BODY: A carbon-oxygen engine built of complex electronic ridges around the genetic entity which animates it.

THE HUMAN MIND: The thetan plus the standard banks.

STIMULUS–RESPONSE: The environment of the thetan activating ridges to make them activate the body.

THE REACTIVE MIND: The ridge automatic response system.

THE SOMATIC MIND: The genetic entity plus the brain system of the body.

SCIENTOLOGY: The science of knowing how to know.

KNOWING HOW TO KNOW: Being the thetan, clear of the body and its ridges and able to handle illusion, matter, energy, space and time.

THETA CLEAR: A being who is reasonably stable outside the body and does not come back into the body simply because the body is hurt. No other condition necessary.

CLEARED THETA CLEAR: A thetan who is completely rehabilitated and can do everything a thetan should do, such as move MEST and control others from a distance, or create his own universe.

A THETAN EXTERIOR: A thetan who is clear of the body and knows it but is not yet stable outside.

SIX LEVELS OF PROCESSING—ISSUE 5
November, 1955

NOTE: Issue Five of the Six Levels of Processing is not the final issue of this operating procedure and is subject to change, especially in the matter of command wording. However, the processes here reproduced have been evolved into a workable state and have been run with success with the commands given. Issue 5 of SLP is released at this time because it is better material, not because it is the final form of SLP.

With SLP is introduced a method of auditing and a new auditing atmosphere which articulates the attitudes best calculated to maintain continuing stable gains in a case. The auditing atmosphere is A-R-C with gain marked by continuing rises in A-R-C. With SLP a somatic or boil-off means reduced A-R-C and are indications of auditing breaks in A-R-C. With SLP comes the *COMMUNICATION BRIDGE*, restarting sessions, maintenance of high Reality, and liberal use of processing outside an auditing room.

All assist type processes are outside SLP except for the present time problem.

The emphasis of SLP is on bettering the preclear's reality and power of choice.

Level One
RUDIMENTS

These must be established at the beginning of every session. They must be re-established each time the preclear tends to go out of session:

(a) *Find the auditor*
(b) *Find the preclear*

(c) *Find the session environment*

(d) *Establish that a session is in progress*

(e) *Accept any communication the preclear originates*

(f) *Acknowledge every command execution by the preclear*

(g) *Agree upon the process and the command form before using and do not confuse it*

(h) *Use two-way communication liberally*

(i) *Follow the Auditor's Code*

(j) *Deal with the present time problem which may be present at the beginning or arise during or re-occur during a session*

(k) *Use a Communication Bridge at every process or area change*

(l) *Establish goals by two-way communication and the command "Assign an intention to————" (auditor indicating object)*

(m) *Run opening procedure of 8-C as given in* The Creation of Human Ability *until the preclear is certainly obeying the auditing commands and is under control.*

Level Two

LOCATIONAL AND NOT-KNOW PROCESSES

Run in populated places, ambulant.

(a) *Energy Sources:*

Have preclear spot acceptable energy sources. Do not permit him to spot statics unless he is ready for it. Run until preclear can empower terminals. Commands: *"Spot an acceptable energy source."*

(b) *Spotting Objects:*

Have preclear spot objects in a place with ample space and objects. Commands: *"Spot an object."*

(c) *Spotting people:*

Have preclear spot people in populated places. Command: *"Spot a person."*

(d) *Separateness from Objects:*

Have preclear spot objects he is separate from, then objects separate from him. Commands: *"Locate an object from which you are separate." "Locate an object which is separate from you."*

(e) *Separateness from People:*

Have preclear spot people he is separate from, then have him spot people separate from him. Commands: *"Locate a person from whom you are separate." "Locate a person who is separate from you."*

(f) *Waterloo Station:*

Have preclear spot people about whom he can Not-Know something and then have him spot people he is willing to have Not-Know things about him. (Auditor selects persons.) Commands: *"Tell me something you wouldn't mind not-knowing about that person." "Tell me something you wouldn't mind that person not-knowing about you."*

Level Three

DECISIONAL PROCESSING

Run in quiet places or auditing rooms.

(a) *Think a Placed Thought:*

The object is to train the preclear to think thoughts exterior to his head and thetan bank to obviate the "cave-in phenomena of Axiom 51." Commands: (auditor indicating object or position) *"Think a thought in (on) that ———."* Alternate command: *"Do you see that (object)? Think a thought in (on) it. Did the thought appear where it is?"*

(b) *Choice Rehabilitation:*

Using the ability acquired in Level Three (a) have the preclear make choices between two objects indicated by auditor. Command: *"From (indicated point) make a choice between (indicated positions or objects)."*

139

(c) *Directed Decision Rehabilitation:*

Using the ability acquired in (a) and (b) exercise the pre-clear on decisions. Command: *"Putting the decision on (in) that (indicated object) make a decision about it."*

(d) *Permissive Decision Rehabilitation:*

Using the abilities acquired in (a), (b) and (c) turn preclear loose on decisions. Decisions must be outside head and bank. Command: *"Decide something."*

Level Four
OPENING PROCEDURE BY DUPLICATION (Not-Know Version)

Done in an auditing room with a book and a bottle.

Commands: *"Do you see that book?"*
"Walk over to it."
"Pick it up."
"Not-know something about its colour."
"Not-know something about its temperature."
"Not-know something about its weight."
"Put it in exactly the same place."
"Do you see that bottle?"
"Walk over to it."
"Pick it up."
"Not know something about its colour."
"Not know something about its temperature."
"Not know something about its weight."
"Put it in exactly the same place."
"Do you see that book?"

Level Five

REMEDY OF COMMUNICATION SCARCITY

The object of this step is to restore abundance on any and all communication possibilities. Done in an auditing room.

(a) *Create confusion:*

Commands: *"Mock up a confusion."* Alternate command: *"What confusion could you create?"*

(b) *Creating Terminals:*

The preclear may have to be coached into mocking up unknown confused black terminals and thus into good terminal mock ups. Commands: *"Mock up a communication terminal." "Mock up another communication terminal."*

(c) *What wouldn't you mind communicating with:*

Duplicate the auditing command exactly. Don't red-herring (go chasing after facsimiles). Command: *"What wouldn't you mind communicating with?"*

(d) *Creating family terminals:*

Have preclear mock up until he has abundance of any and all persons he has ever used as anchor points. Commands: *"Mock up your (father, wife, mother, husband)." "Mock him (her) up again."*

Level Six

REMEDY OF HAVINGNESS AND SPOTTING SPOTS IN SPACE

Route One

An exteriorized step done as given in the Creation of Human Ability.

GAMES PROCESSING

The goal of Scientology is the rehabilitation of the game. The auditor can make a game better or make it possible for the preclear to play a game. The preclear is being audited because he is no longer able to take part in the game. Life is a game consisting of freedom and restrictions. Play is communication. Communication requires freedom and terminals. Life units as-is with thought. To think there must be something to as-is. To grant life there must be something to grant life to. A preclear will become as free as he is reassured of the existence of barriers at that level. When a preclear is not assured of (does not have reality on) barriers at a level he will not rise to that level. A thetan will carry to extremes making something and making nothing. Auditing is that process of bringing a balance between freedom and barriers. A game depends upon a restoration of freedom of choice on making something and making nothing. One can become obsessed with making nothing. He can become obsessed with making something. Both of these activities and the rehabilitation of the freedom of choice bring about a gain in case. There can be too many or too few universes, but when an individual is stuck in a universe it is because he does not have enough universes. Therefore it is necessary to remedy his havingness of bodies. Remedying his havingness of bodies will clear away universes in which he is stuck by letting him have freedom of entrance into universes.

Auditing is a game of exteriorization versus havingness. There is never too much of anything if the preclear is bothered by it. He may say there is not enough of it but he usually says there is something bad about it. When he says there is something bad about it he means there is not enough of it. The preclear loses his power to postulate into existence and to unpostulate out of existence energy masses, spaces and forms.

Life is a game.

Games are composed of freedom, problems, and havingness, awareness and interest.

Each of these elements contains "mood of game" (the tone scale), penalties, and the cycle of action.

Auditing improves the level of game of the preclear.

Auditing is not a game between auditor and preclear on an opposing basis but on a team basis. The auditor, and eventually the preclear, are engaged upon a game, themselves versus the opponents to survival in life.

The preclear is usually close to a no-game condition. This is reached by a preponderance of win (no-game) or a preponderance of lose (no-game). A frozen mood of game or no-mood is reached by assuming that interest can exist on only one emotional level (whereas interest can exist on any emotional tone level) or by misusing the mood of one game in others concurrently played.

A game is any state of beingness wherein exist awareness, problems, havingness and freedom (separateness) each in some degree. A game is rehabilitated or a no-game-condition eradicated in processing by handling the elements of games and their subdivision, with reality, with the intention of bettering the game ability of the preclear.

HAVINGNESS

The Remedy of Havingness

There is a great deal of upper-echelon theory connected with the Remedy of Havingness as a process, for here we are dealing with energy and the reasons and operations of a thetan in regard to it.

Just why a thetan should get himself so completely snarled up in energy might be an entire mystery to anyone who did not realize that a thetan has to cut down his knowingness and his total presence in order to have a game. The awareness of awareness unit builds space to cut down knowingness. Space makes it necessary, then, to look at something in order to know about it. The next thing a thetan does to cut down his knowingness is to create energy and to pass it to other thetans and to bring in the energy of other thetans so as to get a duration and a time-span. If the thetan is successful and obtains a game in this wise, he continues on with this modus operandi of having a game, and when he does not have a game he simply cuts his knowingness down once more. Of course, he reaches a point eventually where he does not get a game simply by cutting down his knowingness, and eventually assumes a fairly fixed, stupid, aspect. He is below the level of having games, but because he has cut down his knowingness he does not know, now, that he is below the level of having games and thinks that all that is necessary to get another game is to further cut down his knowingness. He is by this time obsessively dramatizing the lowering of knowingness.

When one speaks of knowingness, one should realize that one is speaking of an embracive thing. Everything on the Know to Mystery Scale is simply a greater condensation or reduction of Knowingness. At first one simply knows. Then he makes some space and some energy, and so now he has knowingness in terms of looking. By changing the position of the particles of energy thus created, and by exchanging particles with others, extant or self-created, the thetan cuts down his knowingness further, and gets time, and so gets emotion and sensation. When these become solid, he has effort particles and masses. Now, he could cut down his knowingness further by refusing to use emotion and effort, but by thinking about them, thus introducing new vias into his line of knowingness. And, when he no longer knows entirely by thinking, he ceases to create knowingness and begins to eat, and from eating he drops into the ready-made sensation of sex instead of knowing what happens in the future. And from here he drops down into postulated mystery as something one cannot possibly know about. In other words, one gets a continued reduction of knowingness in order to have games. The greatest chess player in the world has no game, since he can predict that he will win and predict everything that opponents will do, so he will simply demonstrate how to play chess. Sooner or later, he will announce that he is "burned out" or has lost his knack for playing chess, and will go off into some other field where he *can* have a game. The field he will choose will be a less wisdom-demanding field than playing chess. A boxer, such as some of the very great ones of the past, will reduce his timing, which is to say his knowingness of arrival, to a point where he can at least put on a good exhibition, and from this they will further reduce their knowingness, and then not noticing how far they have gone, get themselves thoroughly and consistently beaten. There will be a period, however, when they are fairly evenly matched against their opponents.

To understand this with any thoroughness, one would have to recognize the intention back of all communication. Creation, Survival, and Destruction is knowingness. When somebody talks to you his intention is to continue in a parity where he can have an interchange of communication, which is to say a game. He takes knowingness from you, and gives knowingness to you, with one form of communication or

145

another. Two soldiers fighting and shooting at each other are using a bullet to make the other man know. What is there to know in this situation? That one is dead, of course, and for the victor, that one has won.

It is dangerous, alike, to a thetan, to have too many wins or too many losses. Give him too many wins, and he will correct in the direction of reducing his knowingness as represented by his dexterity, his prediction, his activity. Give him too many losses and he will seek another game, even to the point where he will die and pick up another body. Because the decision is on the basis of knowingness, the decision is always downward. One does not decide upward toward greater knowingness, actually, unless one has the full and complete intention of winning in a new game. If one discovers that there are no wins or losses either to be found in this new game, even to the point of forgetting all of his knowledge concerning it, one will reduce one's own knowingness in order to ensure a game.

As there is not an infinity of games in progress, one is apt, as he comes down seventy-four trillion years of track, to play out the available games and to put them in the category of "it must not happen again". One then becomes bored. One is only bored when there is no game possible, from his viewpoint. Actually, all he has to do is become enthusiastic about the game on his own consideration and he will begin to know more about it again.

A thetan considers that some form or mass is necessary in order to have a game. He gets into the belief that he cannot create new masses, and so he begins to hold on to old masses, and here, whether he is exteriorized or in a body, we find him holding on hard to old facsimiles, old significances, old decisions, rather than take on new decisions.

The Remedy of Havingness directly addresses the problems of giving the thetan something 'to play with'. When he discovers that he can have new masses, he will begin to let go of old masses. It is an easily observed phenomenon while having a preclear Remedy Havingness, that old engrams go

146

into restimulation, go into restimulation and run out, that they show up in front of his face and suddenly explode or disappear. The Remedy of Havingness actively does run out engrams.

This process is used from boredom up to conservatism for its best results.

This process is done by asking the preclear to mock up something and pull it in, or mock up something and throw it away. When a thetan is exteriorized, if you want to see him get very unhappy, make him change space until he begins to lose all the energy he is holding on to, and then fail to remedy his havingness. The thetan will become convinced that he is only a thought, and is therefore, by his standards unable to have a game. Tell him to mock up eight anchor points in the form of the corners of a cube around him and pull them in upon himself. Ask him to do it several more times, and he immediately brightens up and becomes very happy. Why is this? You have reassured him that he can have a game.

The cutting down of knowingness and the Remedy of Havingness have opposite vectors. The Remedy of Havingness will knock out old energy masses the thetan is holding on to, or that the body is holding on to, which tell the thetan he is stupid. The supplanting of these by new energy masses which do not have the postulate of cut-down knowingness in them of course makes the thetan brighter.

When you find a theory detached from a process and not demonstrating itself in a process there must be something wrong with the theory. Similarly, if what I say here about condensed knowingness being all other things, and the cut-down of knowingness, were not demonstrated in the process of Remedy of Havingness, then we would have to get ourselves a new theory. However, this is demonstrated very definitely. For those people who cannot remedy havingness wherever they are on the tone scale can be brought to a point where they will remedy havingness simply by asking them what they wouldn't mind knowing. The consideration of what they are willing to know then begins to rise.

147

If you only could see a "black five" operate you would see that his barriers are all erected toward knowing something. Of course he is very afraid of being told something bad, and so doesn't want to be told anything at all, and when the auditor gives him a command he never receives the command as given, but does something else. He has a block up against knowingness to such a degree that he will eventually permit himself to be pressed into complete inactive stupidity. What are those black screens for? Basically to keep him from knowing. Knowing what? Then one will have to look closely at the definition of a datum. A datum is an invention which has become agreed upon and so solidified. In other words, a datum is to some degree a solidity, even if it is merely a symbol. To get into this state it has to be agreed upon. When it is thoroughly agreed upon it becomes, then, a truth. It is not at all a truth. It is an invention. What made it sure or what made it real was the fact that it was agreed upon. This opens the doors further to other processes.

In order to get the preclear in good condition we would have to put him into some kind of a condition so that he could create. The first thing he is liable to be able to create in auditing is a lie. The word lie is simply invention with a bad connotation. Society gives invention that connotation because of its anxiety to have a game and to agree, and so be able to communicate with one another.

Thus society frowns upon the invention of facts, yet the preclear's sanity and continued happiness absolutely depend upon his ability to create new facts. The technique which remedies this is included in "The Creation of Sanity", number R2-29: "Start lying". One can vary this auditing command with "Tell me some lies about your past", and then keep the preclear at it long enough so that the preclear is able to come out of the complete blur which will follow on the heels of his taking over the function of and running of his memory machines. The invention of data is a step immediately toward the remedy of havingness. Simply asking the preclear what he wouldn't mind knowing, what he wouldn't

148

mind having other people knowing about him will bring him into a condition where he can mock up and remedy havingness.

The Remedy of Havingness is the companion process to Spotting Spots, which will be taken up in the next PAB. The Remedy of Havingness, simply as a process by itself, if worked up to by getting the preclear willing to know things, and willing for other people to know things, and run thoroughly so that whole avalanches of masses can pour into him or pour out of him, will actually run out an entire engram bank, and thus is an extremely valuable process.

It has been reported by several auditors that exteriorization was accomplished on preclears by making them remedy havingness and do nothing else for eight or ten hours.

The auditing commands for the Remedy of Havingness are: "Mock up something", "Pull it in", until the preclear is doing this easily. Then,. "Mock up something", "Throw it away", until the preclear can do this easily. The significance of the object may be added by the auditor with "Pull in an ideal body", or some such thing, but the actual fact is that the actual significance does nothing for the preclear. It is the mass which counts. The auditor can have the preclear pull things in two at a time, six at a time. He can have the preclear mock up something, copy it a dozen times, one time after another, then pull in the whole mass, but the real reason he is doing this with the preclear should never drop from sight. The auditor is remedying havingness in order to give the preclear enough mass to permit him to discard old masses which he is holding on to and doesn't know anything about.

Remedy of Havingness—The Process

"When in doubt, remedy Havingness."

This is a motto which can well be followed by an auditor doing any process on the preclear.

149

But, if there is a process which one should do with any other process, then that process would be understood thoroughly, for if done incorrectly it would be likely to produce confusion into all the other processes of Dianetics and Scientology.

Therefore, in the first place, let us examine with rigor the name of this process. It is REMEDY OF HAVINGNESS. By "remedy" one means the correction of any aberrated condition. By "havingness" one means mass or objects. The process could also be called "Remedy of Unhavingness." It could also be called "Remedy of Acceptingness." It could also be called "Remedy of Rejectingness."

To those people who are deficient in Havingness, the process is liable to mean that the auditor should increase the Havingness of the preclear. Such an auditor with the mis-understanding would have the preclear put up large masses and push them into his body or himself. The auditor would neglect having the preclear throw away objects and masses.

If the auditor misunderstood the process and simply assumed that it had something to do with Havingness, and if his own Havingness were too great, he would be likely to specialize on all preclears by having the preclear throw things away.

Actually, the auditor should have the preclear push things into himself and his body and throw things away from himself and his body until the preclear can do both with equal ease. When this has been accomplished the preclear's Havingness has been "remedied".

What, then, does a Remedy of Havingness mean? It means the remedy of a preclear's native ability to acquire things at will and reject them at will. Amongst the Havingnesses which would require remedy, would be an obsessive inflow of money, sexual objects, troubles, somatics, and difficulties in general. Whenever one of these appeared in the preclear's environment it would have a tendency to inflow on the preclear. The reverse difficulty would be an obsessive outflow, whereby the preclear threw away or wasted anything which he had, such as money, clothes, cars, or living quarters. When the process "Remedy of Havingness" has been done thoroughly and completely, the preclear should be able to reject or accept, at his own discretion, anything in his environment as well as anything in the engram bank.

The earliest use of this process is to be found in GITA which is to say "*Give* and *Take* Processing," one of the early SOP's, which became an SOP-8 "Expanded GITA." In Issue 16-G of the Journal of Scientology we have a long list of key items. The preclear was asked to waste, accept, and desire these items at will. This was the Desire-Enforcement-Inhibit Scale, or DEI Scale. This process is the immediate ancestor of the Remedy of Havingness. Indeed, one could do far worse than to take the DEI Expanded GITA list as given in Issue 16-G, and in the form of mock-ups use it as such upon the preclear, or more modernly employ it directly on the Remedy of Havingness on these objects.

If one were to employ such a list in the Remedy of Havingness, one would, of course, have to employ gradient scales. The use of the gradient scale has never been discarded, and the concept and principle of doing things by gradient scales is inherent in auditing itself, for one starts with a process which the preclear can do, and gives him some wins, and on a gradual scale gives him larger and larger wins until he is cleared. Similarly, in remedying Havingness, the preclear must be started at the lowest end of the scale and advanced on up to the higher ends of the scale. Quantity is one of the methods of doing this. At first one can ask a preclear to mock up one of an item and shove it into his body or throw it away, and then go, finally, when he is doing that well, to two items, three, four, five, six, all the same, but a greater quantity of the item. An even lower gradient on this scale would be to simply get the idea that something was there, and to progress on forward with the idea into the actual mass. An expert auditor working with this from the idea on through to the object would discover that he had no preclears who could not mock up.

He would have the preclear get the idea out in front of him of a ball, and get the idea of the ball being thrown away; get the idea of a ball up in front of him and get the idea of a ball coming in. He would then, when the preclear could do this excellently, move forward into the actual mock-up of a ball. The mock-up would get better and better as the process progressed, until at last the preclear could mock up and throw away or push into his body, at will a ball. He would be able to see this ball, even feel its texture and its weight.

Now, exteriorization by Remedy of Havingness is a newer process than the old Remedy of Havingness. It is accomplished by having the preclear SHOVE or PUSH things into his body. One no longer has the preclear PULL things into his body. Simply by having the preclear mock up things and shove them into his body, mock them up and throw them away, mock things up and shove them into his body, mock things up and throw them away, a preclear, who has already been run on the earlier steps of the six basic processes, will, at this stage exteriorize quite neatly after as little as fifteen or twenty minutes of the process. If he does not, then the earlier processes have been skimped and the preclear was really not ready for a full, forthright remedy of Havingness.

Even when doing Route 1, the preclear is told to push things into himself. This will rather take his flitter away for a moment, for he is there being one viewpoint, and in order to push something into himself, he has to be a second viewpoint. In view of the fact that a thetan gets into trouble by being only one viewpoint, this remedies the viewpoint scarcity of the thetan, and he pushes himself up into two viewpoints with great rapidity. Thus we are doing duplication of the thetan at the same time that we are remedying Havingness, so one even has the thetan shove things into himself, rather than pull things into himself.

In short, one never has anyone pull things into his body any more. One has people push things into the body. One has, for instance, the preclear mock up a planet, and push it into the body; mock up a planet and throw it away; mock up a planet and push it into his body; and then one says, "Where are you pushing it from?" The preclear says: "Out here in front of the body." The auditor simply goes on doing the process, and very shortly the preclear will, if the earlier steps have been done well—the Six Basic Processes below Remedy of Havingness—exteriorize neatly and will be ready for Route 1.

One would omit, in such an instance, running Spotting Spots as such, for Change of Space Processing and Communication Processing has a great deal to do with spotting spots already.

If you were to do Remedy of Havingness forthrightly and all-out, and you were to accept this as the only process we had, we would work with its cousin process R2-63 as given in "The Creation of Human Ability," "Accept-Reject." One would ask the preclear for things he could accept, one after the other until the communication lag was flat, and then would ask the preclear for things he could accept, one after the other until the communication lag was flat, and then would ask the preclear for things he could reject, one after the other until the communication lag was flat on that. One would then move into the Expanded GITA list and would have the preclear mock up and shove into his body (if interiorized) or into himself (if exteriorized) the various items on the Expanded GITA list as given in Issue 16-G of the Journal of Scientology. This would be a long process, and not entirely successful on all counts, but would nevertheless be a very effective and efficient process from the standpoint of gain. One would certainly get the preclear over a very large number of aberrations and would do a great deal for him. However, this is not the advised way of handling this process, for the process itself is not an end-all. Aberrations can be handled much more easily by Communication Processing.

The exact use and commands of Remedy of Havingness in ordinary and routine auditing is simple and effective. One has been asking a preclear a great many questions which "as-issed" large masses of energy. One, in handling Change of Space or interiorization and Exteriorization into objects while the preclear is exteriorized, has been "burning up" large masses of energy. Any time the preclear begins to feel dopey or "boil off" he has either run too long on a flow in one direction, in which case reverse the flow, or he has simply reduced his havingness down to a point where he feels tired or sleepy. Without waiting for this manifestation to occur the good auditor simply in the course of Straight Wire or Description Processing, or many other processes, such as those contained in Route One, remedies Havingness. Having achieved something like a momentarily flat communication lag on a process, the auditor says to the preclear: "Mock up a mass out in front of you." When the preclear has done this, the auditor says: "Shove it into your body." When the preclear has done so, the auditor says: "Mock up another mass out in front of you." And when the preclear has done so, the auditor says: "Throw it away." That, as given, is for preclears who are interiorized. It is simply repeated over and over. The mass is not specified. It can be almost anything, and in fact it does not matter much what type of significance the mass has. Any mass is better than no mass, according to the thetan.

If the preclear is exteriorized, the auditor already starts him on the Remedy of Havingness in the Route One step where the preclear is asked to copy what he is looking at (R1-5). When one is doing R1-5 one must be very careful to obey the gradient scale principle behind Remedy of Havingness. One would not make the preclear make twenty copies and then push all of them into himself or the body. One would make the preclear make two or three copies and push them in, one at a time, until the preclear could remedy his Havingness with ease.

The auditor would then have the preclear mock up a mass and "Shove it into yourself." And then: "Mock up a mass

154

and throw it away," and do this back and forth until the preclear could do this easily and well, at which time the auditor would tell the preclear: "Mock up two masses and shove them into yourself," and then, "Mock up two masses and throw them away," until finally the auditor has the preclear mock up eight masses as though they were the corners of a cube around the preclear, and "Shove them into yourself," and then "Mock up eight masses and throw them away."

One must remember that in spite of the fact that he cannot duplicate mass actually as himself, having no space or mass, natively, the motto of the thetan is "anything is better than nothing." When you tear up a lot of facsimiles for a thetan and throw them away, he becomes very unhappy unless you have him reconstruct those facsimiles or remedy the mass according to what he has lost. When you are having a thetan go into and out of MEST universe masses, a certain amount of energy is burned up, and after a thetan has been run for a short time on this step (R1-9 in the "Creation of Human Ability"), one must be particularly careful to remedy his Havingness with eight masses shoved into himself and eight masses thrown away, several times. A thetan who has been run a great deal without Remedy of Havingness comes to what is to him a horrible thought: "I am just a concept", and he will sag in tone. He does not come to this state as long as Havingness is consistently remedied.

It may be, as one looks at Scientology, that one has come to the opinion, watching Remedy of Havingness work, that all there is to anything is the Remedy of Havingness, that it is all based on the Remedy of Havingness. If one has a preclear shove enough Havingness into his body he will exteriorize in most cases. If one remedies enough Havingness while the thetan is chasing around the universe, as in the Grand Tour, the thetan will discover and as-is a great many communication lines which otherwise might be very detrimental. However, it is not true that Havingness is the entire key to the

Human mind. Havingness is the "gimmick" or "weenie" for which the game is played, and having something is very much like winning.

Above Havingness there is Doingness, and above Doingness there is Beingness, and above Beingness there is Communicatingness, and above Communicatingness there is Knowingness, and above Knowingness there is Postulatingness. We see, thus, that we have a long way to go above Havingness in order to get to the top activity of a thetan, which is making postulates or unmaking them.

One could, of course, rationalize each and every action of the thetan with regard to Havingness. One could even extend Havingness to space, although it normally refers to objects. One could do all manner of interesting things with Havingness. One could get as specific and as significant as one likes, or as unsignificant as one likes and still find Remedy of Havingness working, but we do not have here, in Remedy of Havingness, the total clue, total key. But we do have a process and an item which must not be overlooked in auditing.

In the Six Basic Processes, the Remedy of Havingness comes after the Opening Procedure by Duplication as a process, itself, but remember that Remedy of Havingness is done and can be done at any time during any other process as long as the preclear is even vaguely in communication with the auditor. It does not matter how vague the mass is that the preclear is using to remedy his Havingness. Here is a place where certainty is not necessary. An unreal, vague, or flimsy mass, if this is all the preclear can get, will still remedy his havingness.

A case comes to mind out of the Advanced Clinical Course, where a student was unwilling, after his second day, to continue his studies. He did not believe that he could stand the "hammer and pound", as he put it, of the terrifically intense schedule. I took him into my office, asked him what he was doing in life, and he replied to me that he was a machinist. Also, it seemed to turn out that he had something to do with a ship which had sunk under him, although his recollection of this was very unclear. I asked him what kind of a machine he had customarily run, and he told me. Then I had him mock up this machine, and remedied his Havingness with it. Then I had him mock up the ship and remedied his Havingness with that, just as given above. I did this for about fifteen minutes, and enough change occurred in his case to entirely return his confidence in his ability to stand up to the course and to audit. Yet the mockups he was getting were so thin that he could barely vaguely discern them at all.

Mockups get unreal because the thetan is Not-Ising existence. He is trying to destroy masses by saying that they do not exist, that they are not real. He is so bent upon this system of destruction that he is making everything unreal or black. One of the cures for this is End of Cycle Processing run in the following fashion:

One has the preclear mock himself up dead (no matter how unreal the mockup is). Then have the mockup waste away to bone, and have the bones waste away to dust, and then have the preclear shove the dust into himself, or alternately, throw it away. One once more has the preclear mock himself up dead, have the mockup waste away to bone, have the bones waste away to dust, and then have the preclear remedy his Havingness with the dust. One continues this for two or three hours with the preclear if one really wishes the case to make a change. Where a preclear is getting no reality on mockups or blackness he is most commonly stuck in that Para-Scientological thing, that thing horribly abhorred by psychologists who have become Dianeticists, or by people who are just plain scared, a past death. If you wanted to convince somebody that past deaths exist, you would run End of Cycle Processing on them. This is a cousin process to the Remedy of Havingness. One could go a very long distance with this process and have the preclear mock up his mother dead, have her waste away to bones, and remedy Havingness with the dust, or do this with the dust, or do this with the father or brothers, or grandparents, with a considerable change in the case.

This End of Cycle Processing, by the way, is a very fine process. It has been with us about a year and it has been successful whenever used. It has a tendency to fall into disuse because it has not, until now, had an exact place on the Six Basic Processes. But End of Cycle is actually an additional process to the Remedy of Havingness and is an effective way of remedying Havingness. Do you remember in the old days the Dianetics "Corpse Case," who would lie upon the couch with his arms crossed neatly all ready for a lily, and would always audit in this fashion? The solution to this corpse case is End of Cycle Processing, as given here. The preclear is so fixed in a death that he is trying to make everything unreal, and the only real thing, to him, would be the unreality of death.

The Importance of Havingness

A careful study of staff auditors' reports reveals that the only advances worthy of the name of Scientology occur when the auditor repairs or remedies havingness on the preclear. Without the repair and remedy of havingness no real gains become apparent. A preclear will not progress when his havingness is impaired.

What are the symptoms of loss of havingness? Running any as-ising techniques the preclear may become anaten, slightly nervous, agitated, want a cigarette, or seem to break out of the session in some fashion. In either case, he is "down on havingness". In other words he has burned up, used up, or as-ised, too much of his physical body energy in the auditing itself. In view of the fact that every subjective technique puts a sort of hole in the middle of the electronic mass surrounding a preclear, parts of that mass then begin to cave in on the preclear. Thus running an as-ising technique on a preclear beyond the ability of the preclear to sustain the consequent loss of havingness will bring on in the preclear

158

many new engrams which he did not have before. A technique which as-ises energy, if used without a repair or remedy of havingness, will bring about a worsening of the case of a preclear.

Now exactly what is happening is very simple. A preclear starts to go anaten and the auditor keeps on running the process. He hasn't realised that he ought to interrupt a process at any time if the preclear demonstrates a loss of havingness. Anaten is such a demonstration of loss of havingness. All right, another example: the preclear becomes agitated or upset; he reaches for a cigarette; he begins to twitch; his foot begins to wobble; he begins to talk excitedly; he begins to cough while being audited. All of these things demonstrate a loss of havingness. These same conditions by the way, can result from the preclear believing that the auditor has broken the auditor's code in some fashion or has overcome his power of choice. Both a repair and remedy of havingness are immediately indicated on the observation of anaten or agitation on the part of the preclear. In addition the auditor should carefully go over the session itself to find out, if anywhere, the preclear believed his power of choice was being overcome, or if the preclear believed the auditor's code had been broken. You understand that the auditor didn't necessarily have to overcome the preclear's power of choice or break the auditor's code in order that the preclear should believe that this had happened. However, this could be overlooked entirely if the auditor had been careful enough to repair or remedy the havingness of the preclear.

The slightest drop of alertness on the part of the preclear, or the slightest agitation or somatic, should immediately indicate to the auditor that havingness has dropped and must be immediately repaired or remedied. A great deal of time can be spent on the subject of repair and remedy of havingness, and it is time spent with great benefit. It is better to "waste" time spent repairing and remedying havingness than to blunder on through. Now there is another thing I have noticed with regard to this. Auditors are running these days toward cognition. Very well, if they expect a preclear to

159

cognite they should not expect him to pull in a bank upon himself. If an auditor runs a very obvious process which should bring the preclear toward cognition, runs it several auditing commands and then stops and repairs and remedies the preclear's havingness, and then after that asks him the same auditing question two more times, he will discover that he has blown a cognition into view. In other words you could remedy the havingness of a preclear while his mind was on one particular subject and bring a cognition into existence.

This becomes particularly important today, since a few months ago I discovered that you could remedy the havingness of anybody, and I mean just that!! You can remedy anybody's havingness and you can turn on mockups on anybody. In view of the fact that the preclear who has a black field can be caused to mock up blacknesses or invisibilities and shove them into his body brings us into an era of being able to make anybody turn on mockups. By getting the preclear to postulate that the mocked up blackness is bad for the body, will cause that blackness to snap into the body. By getting the preclear to postulate that the invisible mass he has mocked up is bad for the body it will snap into the body. Of course, after this has been done a few times, the consideration of the preclear will change. Then perhaps the blackness or invisibility will only snap in when the preclear postulates that it is good for the body. He may also have a residue left. It is very important to get rid of these repair and remedy of havingness residues. By various postulates such as that the residue is a threat to the body: it is good for the body; it is bad for the body, the residue too will snap in.

Let's differentiate at once here the difference between a repair of havingness and a remedy of havingness. We used to call repair of havingness "giving him some havingness". It needs a better technical term. Therefore let us call this "Repair of Havingness". It means having the preclear mock up anything he can mock up, and in any way it can be done get him to shove (never pull) that mock up into the body, and

160

by similar means to get rid of the residue which went along with the mockup. That is a repair of havingness. *It is a one-way flow; it is an inflow.*

Now a remedy of havingness is getting him to mock up and shove into the body enough masses to bring him to a point where he can eventually throw one away. In other words repair of havingness is simply having him mock up things and have him shove them into the body and a remedy of havingness is having him mock up and shove in and throw away the same type of mock up. Remedy of havingness is always a superior operation to a repair of havingness. Repair of havingness is a very crude stop-gap, but can be used any time. However, a preclear who is working well, and on whom havingness can be remedied, should, at all times, have his havingness remedied, not repaired. In other words any type of mock up should be both shoved into the body and mocked up and thrown away. This should be done in considerable quantity until the preclear is quite relaxed about that particular type of mock up. One does this, remember, every time the attention of the preclear drops, or he becomes agitated.

There is one other little point connected with this which is quite important, and that is auditors very often audit a preclear into an area of time when the preclear exteriorised. This, on a preclear who does not exteriorise easily, brings on a considerable grief and sadness. The way to get rid of this is, of course, to remedy the preclear's havingness or only repair it, and to ask the preclear to *recall times when he was not exteriorised*. This will bring up at once times when he did exteriorise and where fear of exteriorisation was built up considerably.

I have noticed another special condition regarding this exteriorisation phenomena which is quite important. A preclear will occasionally repair and remedy havingness up to a point where the body disappears for him. He doesn't quite know where to put the mass he has mocked up since he cannot find the body. This is particularly true of preclears

161

who have a very low threshold on havingness. An auditor would be stupid indeed to simply plow along beyond *that point where the preclear has already said that he* couldn't find any body to push any havingness into. The moment the preclear does that the auditor should suspect that the preclear has gotten into an exteriorisation type incident. It is not, however, necessary that he immediately flounder around and try to find this incident as recommended in the paragraphs just above. He can also repair and remedy havingness in this fashion, and it is very important to know this. Although it is disastrous for a preclear to be asked "What could your body have," since he will simply strip the bank of various old facsimiles, it is a very, very good repair of havingness to ask a preclear *"What is there around this room (area) which your body could have,"* and then have him pick out specific objects in the environment which he says the body could have. If he does this he will come up the gradient scale of havingness, and his havingness will be repaired immediately or directly on the Sixth Dynamic. A preclear who cannot get mock ups and where the auditor has either been too clumsy to get the preclear's mock ups turned on, or it really was impossible, more or less, the preclear's havingness can be repaired by having him do this process. So this is a very, very important process, and one that ought to go down in red letters.

This whole subject of repair and remedy of havingness and its effect upon auditing, and the fact that it has not been stressed at all in training, being up there at level six in the old Basic Processes, brings us to SLP Issue 8. The entirety of level one in SLP 8 will be devoted to the repair and remedy of havingness.

In SLP Issue 7 we have a great many phenomena associated with the remedy of the body's havingness. The reason for their position is to bring about an adjustment of the condition of the body before one goes on to other and more complicated ways of processing. Now, in Issue 8, all of these various things will be retained, but they will be

162

paralleled with a complete remedy of havingness and that particular level of SLP will be gone over. In actual experience it is better to remedy the havingness of a preclear, no matter where he is on the tone scale, and no matter by what process, than to run any significant process. Further, if a preclear cannot at least repair his havingness, to run Waterloo Station is to invite disaster because in this particular process of level 2 he is liable to get himself into a "down havingness" situation and of course will not be able to not-know anything. He may be chewing up too much energy or trying to not-know. Thus we would have the failures which have occasionally occurred in Waterloo Station. They were simply havingness failures, not a failure of Waterloo Station. Further there has been a new command suggested for Waterloo Station: *"What would you be willing to not-know about that person?"* This seems to be a better command, at least for the British Isles.

We also take care of the vacuums and separatenesses and everything else with repair or remedy of havingness and running it in with certain other things, such as problems, etc. When we discover by two-way communication a weak universe, we could then ask the individual preclear *"Invent a problem that person (weak universe) could be to you."* Then, watching him very carefully, and repairing his havingness on the subject of that person's possessions, get a very rapid separation of universes. I have noticed that the weak universe came about when the person elected by the preclear to be a weak universe first began to put mest anchor points around the preclear. In other words, valuable presents. I am as pleased as can be to get a finger on this point and I know well that if east, west, north and south, would begin to repair and remedy havingness, and stop specialising in significances, without repair or remedy of havingness, we are going to start shooting people up to the top of these Scientometric graphs. We can't help it. Let me call your attention specifically to the old phenomena of the emotional scale and the engram. We find out that when one engram was keyed in it fixed the

163

emotional tone of the individual. Then we had him run this and as he converted the engram to usable havingness, we found that his tone rose. We discover on these Scientometric charts that the "unhappy" section does not move if we don't change the mass of the preclear.

Sacrifices

The latest news from the research front has to do with the fact that the GE demands and requires and has to have, evidently, sacrifices. The GE does not run on an overt act-motivator sequence, which makes one suspect he is not a thetan. A GE runs exclusively on being sacrificed to. If you have the preclear mock up sacrifices to the GE, you will find these become very readily assimilated. On a lower level the body accepts motivators; as soon as it is through this motivator band, it accepts sacrifices and finally comes up to a point where it will accept live bodies. When one considers that eating is entirely a matter of absorbing death, one sees this death hunger in processing by running Sacrifices. A person who has had bad legs should have a sacrifice of legs run on him and so forth. This is astonishing material. It is almost unbelievable that the GE will not be sacrificed to anything, but will only be sacrificed to, and this phenomenon that the GE is thereby demanding death tells us at once that the Atomic Bomb will be used and that there are people in the world who will actually crave this sacrifice of cities and even nations. Aside from being a fantastically workable process, more of which anon, this matter of sacrifices tells us at once a great deal about the future. There will be no moral restraint where the Atomic Bomb is concerned. For about the highest level in some areas of the world is, to case, "operating GE." This tells us, too, why soldiers will go to war. This explains a great deal of conduct. The GE evidently operates on the postulate that as long as anything else is alive it can't live. However, it is becoming more and more doubtful that there is any more life in the body than the thetan puts there, and that the body is a single machine operating on some implanted postulate contained in the energy masses which are activated by the thetan somewhat on the order of the old "pole" theta trap. Many of these considerations can be changed around rather easily. Nothing changes them quite so fast as these sacrifice processes. In mocking up sacrifices the auditor should use all the skills of creative processing and ensure that the preclear is actually mocking up and is not dragging in old facsimilies from the bank and restimulating genetic line incidents. This can be obviated by having the persons in the mock ups dressed in modern clothing; mocking up the incident as happening tomorrow; altering the mock up in some manner, such as turning the face green or something of this nature. Any reasonable way in which you can ensure that you are dealing with mock ups and not past track facsimilies.

This gives auditors another tool with which to handle chronic somatics.

There is another process which has a great deal of workability with chronic somatics. I know that some months ago and earlier than that it seemed rather fatal to us to continue to fixate the preclear's attention on the chronic somatic. But that is not a problem with us right now. It ceased to be a problem the moment I invented an auditing command exactly as follows: *"Invent a problem that (leg, arm, nose, eye, body) could be to you."* Running this command, which is in itself a sort of remedy of havingness, and repairing and remedying the havingness of the preclear as we go, we will discover that practically any and all phenomena associated with the service facsimilie will come away and clear up and the limb, nose or eye will get well. This can be used as a word of warning: ONLY ON ACTUAL TERMINALS. Never use this command, and I mean NEVER, on actual conditions. Never ask him to invent problems lameness could be to him. Never ask him what problem blindness could be to him. Lameness and blindness are conditions. We want to know what problems *legs* or *eyes* can be to him, since legs and eyes are terminals. In running this command we reduce havingness too rapidly whenever we are stressing conditions. Therefore we run it only on terminals. In running it use only terminals. Handled in this way we do have the answer as of this moment, to chronic somatics. With these processes in SLP and the adequate repair and remedy of havingness we can push our preclears right up through the top.

ORDER YOUR BOOKS FROM
THESE CHURCHES
OF SCIENTOLOGY

UNITED STATES

WASHINGTON, D.C.
The Founding Church of Scientology
2125 "S" Street N.W.
Washington, D.C. 20008

LOS ANGELES
Church of Scientology of California
New American Saint Hill
2723 West Temple Street
Los Angeles, Calif. 90026

Church of Scientology of California
The New Los Angeles Organization
2005 West 9th Street
Los Angeles, California 90006

Church of Scientology
Advanced Organization
916 South Westlake
Los Angeles, Calif. 90006

Church of Scientology
Celebrity Centre
1551 North La Brea Ave.
Hollywood, Calif. 90028

SAN FRANCISCO
Church of Scientology of California
414 Mason Street
San Francisco, Calif. 94102

SACRAMENTO
Church of Scientology of California
819 19th Street
Sacramento, California 95814

BOSTON
Church of Scientology
of Boston
448 Beacon Street
Boston, Mass. 02115

ST. LOUIS
Church of Scientology of Missouri
3730 Lindell Blvd.
St. Louis, Missouri 63108

DETROIT
Church of Scientology of Michigan
19 Clifford
Detroit, Mich 48226

AUSTIN
Church of Scientology of Texas
2804 Rio Grande
Austin, Texas 78705

SEATTLE
Church of Scientology of Washington
1531 4th Avenue
Seattle, Wash. 98101

LAS VEGAS
Church of Scientology of Nevada
2108 Industrial Road
Las Vegas, Nev. 89102

MIAMI
Church of Scientology of Florida
1235 Brickell Avenue
Miami, Florida 33131

MINNEAPOLIS
Church of Scientology
of Minnesota
730 Hennepin Avenue
Minneapolis, Minn. 55403

NEW YORK
Church of Scientology of New York
30 West 74th Street
New York, New York 10023

BUFFALO
The Church of Scientology
New Buffalo Organization
1116 Elmwood Avenue
Buffalo, New York 14222

HAWAII
Church of Scientology of Hawaii
143 Nenue Street
Honolulu, Hawaii 96821

SAN DIEGO
Church of Scientology of San Diego
926 "C" Street
San Diego, Calif. 92101

PORTLAND
Church of Scientology of Portland
333 South West Park
Portland, Ore. 97205

PHILADELPHIA
The Church of Scientology of Philadelphia
8 West Lancaster Ave.
Ardmore, Penn 19003

CHICAGO
The Church of Scientology of Chicago
1555 Maple
Evanston, Ill. 60201

CANADA

TORONTO
Church of Scientology of Toronto
124 Avenue Road
Toronto, Ontario, Canada
M5R 2H5

OTTAWA
Church of Scientology
292 Somerset W.
Ottawa, Ontario, Canada
K2P 9Z9

MONTREAL
Church of Scientology
15 Notre Dame Ouest
Montreal, Quebec, Canada
H2Y 1B5

VANCOUVER
Church of Scientology of British Columbia
4857 Main Street
Vancouver, British Columbia
Canada V5V 3R8

ENGLAND

Hubbard College of Scientology
Saint Hill Manor
East Grinstead
Sussex, England RH19 4JY

Church of Scientology of Manchester
48 Faulkner Street
Manchester M1 4FH

LONDON
The Hubbard Scientology Organization
68 Tottenham Court Road
London W1, England

PLYMOUTH
Scientology Plymouth
39 Portland Square
Sherwell, Plymouth, Devon

SCOTLAND

EDINBURGH
H.A.P.I. Scotland Fleet House
20 Southbridge
Edinburgh 1, Scotland

DENMARK

COPENHAGEN
Church of Scientology of Denmark
Hovedvagtsgade 6
1103 Copenhagen K

Church of Scientology of Copenhagen
Fredericksborgvej 5
2400 Copenhagen NV
Denmark

Church of Scientology
Advanced Organization
and Saint Hill
Jernbanegade 6
1608 Copenhagen V
Denmark

SWEDEN

Church of Scientology of Sweden
Magasinsgatan 12
S-411 18 Goteborg, Sweden

MALMO
Church of Scientology of Malmo
Skomakaregatan 12
S-211 34 Malmo, Sweden

STOCKHOLM
Scientology Kyrkan
Kanmakaregatan 46
S-111 60 Stockholm, Sweden

HOLLAND

Scientology Kerk Nederland
261 Singel
Amsterdam C, Holland

GERMANY

Scientology Munchen
8000 Munchen 2
Lindwurmstrasse 29
Munich, Germany

FRANCE

Church of Scientology of Paris
12 rue de La Montagne Ste.
Genevieve, 75005 Paris, France

SOUTH AFRICA

JOHANNESBURG
Church of Scientology
of South Africa (Pty.) Ltd.
99 Polly St.   Johannesburg,

PORT ELIZABETH
Church of Scientology
2 St. Christopher's
27 Westbourne Rd.
Port Elizabeth, S. Africa 6001

CAPETOWN
Church of Scientology of
South Africa (Pty.) Ltd.
Garmor House   127 Plein Street
Capetown, South Africa

DURBAN
Church of Scientology in
South Africa (Pty.) Ltd.
College House 57 College Lane
Durban, South Africa

PRETORIA
224 Central House
Cnr. Central & Pretorius Streets
Pretoria, South Africa

AUSTRALIA

ADELAIDE
Church of Scientology 57 Pulteney St.
Adelaide 5000,
So. Australia

MELBOURNE
Church of Scientology
724 Inkerman Road
North Caulfield 3161
Victoria, Australia

SYDNEY
Church of Scientology
1 Lee Street
Sydney 2000, New South Wales

PERTH
Church of Scientology
Pastoral House
156 St. George's Terrace.
Perth 5000,
W. Australia

NEW ZEALAND

AUCKLAND
Church of Scientology
of Auckland
Suites 1-4, 2nd Floor
Imperial Building
44 Queen Street
Auckland 1, New Zealand

RHODESIA

BULAWAYO
508 Kirrie Bldgs.
Abercorn Street
Bulawayo, Rhodesia